YOU SHALL RECEIVE POWER

AND YOU SHALL BE. . .

YOU SHALL RECEIVE POWER
AND YOU SHALL BE. . .

Chas Stevenson

Stevenson Ministries

Published by:
STEVENSON MINISTRIES
PO Box 421236, Houston, TX 77242
www.stevensonministries.org

Book design, cover design, interior design by Stevenson Ministries
Editors: Joni Stevenson, Delia Prince

Published in the United States of America

ISBN: 978-0-578-10341-9

Dedication

"Evangelist Angelo Mitropoulos, Signs and Wonders Evangelism" was the advertisement at my home church for the coming weekend of meetings. My heart leaped when I read it, because I was interested in that, and I had just left my business career for the ministry. I had been praying for sick people and seeing many of them instantly healed. And I had been trying to share my faith effectively with others. But as I watched this certain Greek-turned-American preacher, my vision of God's power went to a new place. During the meetings, I watched a breast cancer patient stand at the front of the church to be prayed for, follow the command to go check herself in the restroom, and return with no sign of it. I watched another elderly lady that I knew personally, racked with arthritis, run around the building totally pain free. I thought to myself, *I knew it! I knew that's what the gospel of Jesus could do!* During the meetings, I also noticed something else. I listened to this preacher tell of how he went to Chicago with a loud speaker on his van and preached to the downtown pedestrians for a month. He said that he estimated that at least one million Chicagoans heard his amplified gospel, and that his voice got so strained that he finally recorded himself on cassette, put the microphone near the van speakers, and sat outside his van while the recording preached to the people. I watched him give our small church 15,000 gospel tracts to saturate our community with the Word of God. And I said to myself, *This preacher actually believes in saving souls!* And so do I.

That began a relationship of teacher, student, partner, and friend between us that lasted until Angelo departed for his crown in heaven. For many years, I worked with Angelo in churches, in the streets, in the tent meetings, and in the print shop printing tracts, doing whatever was needed to get just one more sinner saved or one more believer trained in witnessing, healing the sick, and seeing many mighty miracles along the way. Angelo let me into his life, imparted everything he could about God, this gospel, and the anointing of the Spirit. And, I am forever grateful.

Angelo was a kind man who never met a stranger. He was unique, special, funny, exciting, and he mightily shook every congregation he preached to. He was a devoted father of five and a committed husband. He was totally in love with the Lord Jesus, his heavenly Father, and the Church. And he was a visionary who was totally sold-out to the great commission of bringing people to Christ. Angelo was the most pure and powerful evangelist I have ever known. And this book is a dedication to him—my teacher, my partner and my friend.

Table of Contents

PART 2
Strategy, Mechanics, Theology

INTRODUCTION

THE CALL OF THE CHRISTIAN can only be understood and fulfilled if we first travel backward in time through the history of the Christian. There was a time when the believer was not a believer, when the follower of Christ was following the world. And there was a certain pathway to the Lord that each person who is saved traveled upon, each pathway being different.

The most beautiful thing that has ever happened to a Christian is that he was born again. Or it may be the day that he repented from years of backsliding. The path is narrow and the gate is straight, and what a glorious thing to be on the path and right with God. We rejoice and are glad about the abundant life we've received from Christ. But then we must think back to how we reached that narrow pathway. Once we see our progression to God, we realize that it was lined with Christians who influenced us—one or more, little or lots, someone else helped us reach the Lord. And this is where we begin to recognize *the call of the Christian.*

It is true. After we believe, we are to help others do the same. We cannot neglect this call, only rejoicing that we, ourselves, have been saved and healed and renewed by the Spirit. How selfish it would be to forget our path to God, which was made possible only by the perfectly positioned *other believers* who presented us with the truth. *We have now become one of them.* It is said that even the most introverted person will influence approximately 10,000 people in their lifetime in various ways. I believe God wants us—no, *needs* us—to influence them toward Him. The desire we have had to share Christ with others is real. It is from heaven. It is the nature of God. It came the day the Spirit of God moved into our hearts. It is the purpose of Jesus Christ. He came to seek and save that which was lost (Luke 19:10); and He is still seeking those that are lost. The Lord Jesus has a goal: to give God another house to dwell within—not a church building, but a temple made without hands—a person. But He is limited in his task, as He can only reach *outside people* through His *inside people*. He is reliant upon our obedience. He is reliant upon our compassion for people and our zeal to reproduce ourselves. And we must not faint.

To the Christian who is uncertain of his purpose on earth; to the Christian who has not felt that zeal to help someone repent and believe in the Lord; to the Christian who longs to fulfill this heavenly call of duty with power and confidence, this book is for you. Each chapter will impart something into your soul that will help you see things more spiritually, more eternally, and more clearly. You'll be inspired to something holy and real, and you will get the faith and fire you need to do your part in this awesome commission. Our labor of love matters. Eternity's next phase begins soon, so we've got to do spiritual things right. If we hear, from our Lord, the words, "Well done, thou good and faithful servant..." rather than just a "Well?", we'll be glad we answered the call of the Christian.

If you have fear of this, or if you have previously failed or found it frightening, don't be afraid. We all have had that hindering fear, but it cannot be the final word on the matter. The power to share the gospel is *more* real, and that is where this book will take you. There are some things to learn. There are some things to avoid. Training and practice are involved in sharing our faith. And we need some inspiration. The early disciples were inspired and trained personally by Jesus. Now, we can be personally trained by the Holy Spirit. And we can be motivated and trained by the ministers of God. I want to give you the secrets of being a Spirit-filled, compassionate witness for the Lord. And I want to teach you how to zero in on the people who are ready and lead them to confess Christ as Lord and Savior. There are many ways to help fulfill the great commission of evangelizing the world. And in this book, you will certainly find something that works for you, something that will anchor you with confidence, even some things that surprise you, free you, and fire you up to serve God. No longer can we continue to think that the preachers are to win all the souls. The preachers are given to affect the *saved*, so that the *saved* can better affect *the unsaved*.

As you read this book, I want you to recognize something very important—that the personal triumphs and stories that I share are not as an evangelist, but as a Christian—no special anointing, no unique ability—just a real believer sold out to the call. I realize some people don't feel spiritual enough to participate in this great spreading of the gospel. But if you'll allow me to charge you with divine purpose and insight, you too can join in the holy excitement of building of God's kingdom.

Not fulfilling the call of God to reconcile people to Him will cause the Christian's heart to subtly, silently nag him. Complacency in sharing Christ will cause the life of God to remain bottled up inside him so that he is never renewed day by day since there is nothing to renew. The Christian must not become like the Dead Sea, which receives from the Sea of Galilee by the river Jordan, but has no exit rivers flowing out of it. It is stagnant, unhealthy, and dead. Stagnant life ruins what it has. Revive yourself. Revive the world. Let your light so shine. Confess Christ to all, that He will confess you to God. Get ready, for you're about to hear heaven's great trumpet call, *the call of the Christian*.

Part 1

Get Inspired and Get Moving

1
Whoo Hoo! I'm Saved!

One day in downtown Philadelphia I visited a mall to spend some leisure time. Afterwards, I was outside on the sidewalk and noticed a very sad looking young man sitting on the bench. I went and sat by him and opened up a conversation about the Lord. He looked up at me and seemed really open to what I was saying. He acknowledged his state of depression and rehearsed some of the reasons for his hopelessness. He even described how he had attended church a few times somewhere, but that he didn't have any relationship with God and felt the burden of guilt inside him. I assured him that if he would open up and allow Jesus to enter his life, the light of God would be on his soul and his future would brighten up. He believed the brief words I shared, and he prayed to receive Jesus right there. As soon as he finished praying and dried his eyes, he looked up at me and started smiling—even laughing a bit. He said, "I feel it. I got it. I'm okay now. Thank you so much." And he jumped up from the bench and took off running down the busy sidewalk shouting, "I'm saved! I'm saved! I'm saved! I'm saved! Jesus Christ saved me! Whoo hoo!" He turned around once as he jumped up in the air, waved to me, and ran off praising and leaping with his hands in the air. And that was the last I ever saw of him.

All he needed was a sincere Christian to take a simple moment and share a simple gospel. And his life was changed forever. What motivated me to talk to him? Jesus' last words.

> **Go ye into all the world, and preach the gospel to every creature. He who believes and is baptized will be saved** (Mark 16:15).
>
> **Go ye therefore, and teach all nations** (Matthew 28:19).

Jesus' entire ministry on earth culminated in these last words. Out of all the final things He could have said, this was it. The Lord Jesus did *not* say "Go ye and pray every day", even though we are Christians, and we should. He did *not* say "Go be good and worship God", even though we are Christians, and we should. Instead, he reiterated our work assignment. Yes, our spiritual *work*. And please don't close the book because I mentioned it. 'Work' is not a bad four letter word.

I know we're frequently reminded that first we are *to be*, rather than *to do*—that *being* precedes the *doing*. I get that, and I agree. We can't let our busyness, even if it is for the Lord, cause us to neglect what comes first— *being, abiding, living in Him*. But we have to admit that *the doing* is a big part of life, and for the rest of our lives, we'll be doing a lot of it. I believe Jesus wanted a say-so in our *doing*. And if we'll just take his final words literally, we can have an immediate re-ordering of our priorities. Though there are many things that Christians can do and should do, what Jesus emphasized as His final command was the *reaching out* part we are to do *outside*—outside the assembly and outside our prayer closet. I believe it was because He knew how easy it would be for Christians to get so side-tracked with church activities and *inside stuff* that they would

> **WITNESS PRINCIPLE 1**
>
> Jesus' Last Words

forget the lost world around them. Sharing Christ with the lost will keep your spirit tender before the Lord. And a church that majors on its people sharing Christ with the lost will also stay tender before the Lord.

Notice that if praying, praising, and worshipping were our only tasks, we could go to heaven and do that. The very day that we were born again, we could have been raptured up to heaven by God with His greeting of, "You made it! You got born again! Welcome to heaven! I'm so proud of you!" But, we weren't, and He didn't! He left us in the middle of this sinful world with one purpose: *bring more with you.* Two things we can do on earth that we can't do in heaven are: sin and share Christ with a sinner. Don't sin. But do share Christ with a sinner.

It is clear from Scripture that our Church family is of utmost importance in our life, and we must be dedicated to our fellow believers and our local church above all else, for it is the Body of Christ—Christ Himself. But if we think about it, we are outside the church assembly more hours of the week than we are in it. And while we are out, the Lord Jesus expects us to go after people. We have all been told to "Go." Not necessarily "Go into full time ministry," but rather, "Go to your neighbor, your friends, *your* people in *your* world." We know that Satan's ambassadors are going. We know that hell's forces are going after the world to keep people dark and afflicted. So, if we don't go, the world has no light, leaving hell to rejoice in its triumph.

It's as if the boss of the company is leaving for a long trip. Before he leaves, he gives his administrative assistant one final, paramount instruction during his absence, "While I'm gone, be sure to mail this package. It is the main thing."

"Sure thing, boss."

After a long while, the boss comes back and asks for a status report on the company, "What happened while I was gone?" And the administrative assistant replies, "Well, I made many changes in the office here. I rearranged the cubicles, I finally cleaned up the filing system. And you'd be so proud, I didn't let anyone into your office."

"But what about the package? Did you mail it?"

"Oh, wait, here is the best of all. I instituted a once a week 'happy day' here at the company to keep everyone excited and entertained so they wouldn't leave for one of our competitors. And I hung a pretty picture of you in the foyer so everyone would remember you."

"But the package, did it get mailed?"

"Uh, well, I was kind of busy, boss. And well, uh, you know how difficult that postal office can be. And uh, well, I'm sorry, it seems I did a lot of good things, but not that thing. Was that the main thing?"

"Yes. That was the main thing."

I believe that His final command is the one He wanted ringing in our ears until His return. I believe it is His top priority. The other stuff we do comes more naturally, so He knew we'd do some of it. His final words were not, "Be a good person, take care of your family, and go to church every week." Rather, his final command was to address something that we wouldn't naturally do. It requires some emphasis. It is the mission of the Church—our *one* assignment, and it should be the mission of the individual believer. It is called a *co*mmission because it's been authorized by another. Jesus has commanded it and delegated it. And we need an attitude about it. An attitude of personal soul-winning and world evangelism should be the heartbeat of every believer. Though there are many wonderful things to learn of God, to receive from God, and to do for God, we must be in synch with God's heartbeat. We must take heed not to be sidelined with *getting*. You know, we have found great and precious promises that reveal things we can get from God, like salvation, joy, peace, healing, prosperity, success, and more. But if the Christian spends most of his time trying to *get*, there is a problem. Christians have been commanded to *give*. *Getting* always emphasizes 'self', but *giving* is the nature of God's love, and it emphasizes others. When we turn into a *giver* of joy, of peace, of money, of goodness, of blessing, and yes—of salvation, we begin to match the rhythm of God's heartbeat, which, if you could hear it, would thump ... *souls souls... souls souls... souls souls.* It is the main thing. And it should be the main thing to every single Christian.

2
There Are Giants in the Land

Do you have the gift of soul-winning? Of course you don't, because there is *no such thing*. Never once does the Bible mention a "gift of sharing your faith" or "gift of being a witness" or "gift of soul-winner." There is the gift of the Holy Spirit. And there is a gift of the evangelist, but an evangelist is different from a soul-winner. An evangelist is one of the five specific preaching gifts given to edify the *Church* and to perfect the *saints*. Though evangelists have a special ability to preach to crowds of sinners with results of miracles and salvations, their dual purpose includes preaching to the Church to keep it burning to fulfill the great commission of Jesus Christ. And they will always be graced with the ability to captivate and edify a group or crowd. On the other hand, a soul-winner is any Christian who has obeyed the command of Jesus to be a witness, "And you shall receive power after the Holy Spirit has come upon you, and you shall be witnesses unto me…" (Acts 1:8).

Though most believers aren't called to be an evangelist and preach to a crowd, we are all called to share our faith—to be a witness. And we all can do it because the Spirit has given us power. Every one of us can talk one to one, face to face, with someone else about Jesus Christ.

What is a *witness*? It is someone who has knowledge relevant to an event or other matter of interest and is compelled to testify. One Bible translation says "*you shall be living proof of Me.*" God needs Christians to show and tell the world that sin is paid for and Jesus is alive. He needs Christians to be the living proof that it's all real. Witnessing is a simple conversation between a Christian and a lost person about this great salvation plan. Any Christian can do it.

What has happened to the Church is that we tried to separate a couple of Christian callings and turn them into *special* Christian callings that not everyone has. Prayer and witnessing have been the targeted activities. In our modern churches, we have formed the prayer warrior team and the soul-winning team, and they usually turn out to be a small, select number of enthusiastic Christians. Then they are told that that is their special gift and that very few are selected for these groups. But the New Testament scriptures don't ever refer to prayer and witnessing as special ministry callings. Actually, if we are really teaching perfection in Christ, then each and every Christian is to be both a great praying person and also a great witnessing person. But, if we separate these groups out as a special ministry calling, we effectively relieve other Christians who have not yet excelled in those areas from their Christian duty. Sincere Christians ought to be enthusiastic, and we ought to use our faith to break through any dull spiritual feelings about *both* praying and witnessing. That is what pleases the Lord.

For too long, pulpits have allowed us to think that the soul-winners are the select few church members who do that scary, dirty "street ministry" and go into prisons and downtown areas to win souls. I am not at all against ministering in the streets nor going into the prisons, nor in churches setting up teams and events to do so. But this book is not about that. If you never went out with the street team, that is fine with me. But I want to put an end to *the rest of the church feeling exempt from the evangelism process because they don't "have the special gift, grace, or call."* We are all called to share Christ with others.

We all come to Christ with very different personalities, strengths, and weaknesses. Some of us are extroverts, some aren't. Some like to talk a lot, some don't. Some are more naturally courageous and open. Some aren't. But with this new life in Christ, something happens on the inside of us—a deposit of God's power and nature takes up residence in us. Once this happens, the Holy Spirit can then use us to touch people. The beauty of the Spirit *within* is to bring our inward man *out*. It is not our personality that touches people. It is not our cleverness or our professionalism that touches people's heart. And it's not our loud mouth. It is the Spirit. As long as our spirit man is able to reach outside the scope of our soul (ourselves), then we can help others. But if our outward man is too hard, too crusty, too scared, or too self-centered, our inward man remains locked up inside. If you'll open your heart to this plan and command of God, your faith will grow enough to break the outward man and let the power and love inside you flow out.

(By the way, I said that I was perfectly okay with you not going out with the soul-winning street team. However, in my experience with many first timers, if you did accompany the street team, you'd be extremely blessed and would probably get free from your fears much quicker. Watching someone else always helps.)

The truth is this: the first thing that stops people from sharing Christ is not a lack of special gifting. Rather, it is because "*there are giants in the land.*" Just like with Israel, our "promised land of spiritual success" is just beyond the river Jordan. But we can't have it without killing the giants who live there. What giant do we face in witnessing? Fear. The lack of confidence, the fainting determination to obey, and the worry of what we might encounter is the first roadblock to us believers sharing our faith. It is a roadblock to the gospel reaching the world. And it is of the devil. The intimidation, the embarrassment, and the dread of being rejected are hindrances for the Christian. And about ten out of twelve believers, just like Israel's spies who tucked their tails, balk at it, because of this fear. There is only one way to beat it. It is to *do* it. Not one of us is born again with an immediate, 100% confidence in sharing our belief with someone else. There is no *gift* of witnessing. Rather, we must respond to both the instruction of our Lord, and also that desire deep down that is innate from the Holy Spirit. He wants us to tell everyone. So that's what we make ourselves do. Faith is not a feeling, but an action. We don't *feel* fearless before we act on our faith. We act by faith, *then* we feel fearless.

> **WITNESS PRINCIPLE 2**
>
> Killing the Giant of Fear

When I came back to God as an adult, I knew that being a Christian included telling everyone else about Him. So I tried. I told all my friends, all my family, and anyone else who would listen. But I was scared doing it. I didn't know much, but I knew the right thing was to share this great salvation with others. At this time in my life, I was a business systems consultant and traveled constantly. Every Monday, my company would fly me to my assigned out of town client. And every Friday, they would allow me to fly back home for the weekend. I did this for over a year. Going *to* the airport, I always used one particular town car service and had the same driver every week. But coming home *from* the airport, I always just hailed the next taxi-cab. And there I sat, alone in the car with one stranger for 45 minutes. But you know how it is, the mind starts rehearsing that old—every Christian has it—spirit vs. flesh thought war, *What am I going to do? Should I tell him something? Should I not? He's probably saved anyway. What if he's not? What if he is mean? He probably doesn't like talking about religion. And if I do, the whole trip will be uncomfortable. But what if he needs Jesus? What if I don't tell him and he has a car crash tomorrow and dies, and it's on me? What if God just wants me to try?* The first couple of months, this would go on for about 40 of the 45 minutes, and finally, just before entering my neighborhood, I would muster up the courage to say something about God. "Sir, do you believe the Bible?" Or, "Do you know anything about Jesus Christ?" And every time I opened the conversation, the driver would begin to talk, and I would get to share Christ. I only knew a couple of scriptures and had only one message. So that's what I shared. My message for everyone was John 14:6—that Jesus is the only way to the Father—that neither Muhammad, nor Bhudda, nor Mary, nor good works, nor any religious tradition could get a person to God. And every time I did it, I felt so good afterward. I did it every week. I was also being a shining light at work, and being a good example of love to those I knew. But I always knew Friday would come and I would be with a stranger that I had to talk to. And feelings of dread and worry would come over me. But every Friday, at the last moment of my ride, I would obey God.

After a couple of months, however, things began to change. I was able to gradually shorten my "struggle-time" and find the courage to speak sooner about the Lord. Finally, at about the five month mark, I calculated that out of all my witnessing, not one taxi cab driver had received Jesus. A few people had asked for prayer for various things, but no one had responded fully. So what did that mean? Absolutely nothing. Had I failed? Absolutely not. By that point, I had learned enough about God's Word to know that no gospel seed planted is a failure. But just as important was the other thing I realized: *I was free.* I had overcome the fear of witnessing. I had confidence and boldness to help others know the truth, and I was no longer afraid at all. How did I know? Because each Friday, I would start talking about Jesus before we ever left the airport terminal. I didn't have to struggle for 40, 30, or even 20 minutes. I could open up a conversation about God immediately and then have the entire trip to talk to them if the Spirit opened them up. And I have been free ever since. Of course, back then I still hadn't learned how to zero in quite as efficiently, and I have grown in wisdom. But those first few months were my fight of faith against the giant of fear. And I won. If you will earnestly desire to be a living proof of Jesus, you too can overcome the fear.

3

Out–Witnessed by a Five Year Old

Whosoever desires to come after Me, let him deny himself, and take up his cross, and follow Me. For whoever desires to save his life will lose it, but whoever loses his life for My sake *and the gospel's* will save it (Mark 8:34-35).

To be a follower of Christ, there is an element of surrender where we give up our self-centered life in order to have Christ's life. Our desires for pleasure, for comfort, for fame, and for the 'American dream', and for honor before man, and all of our pride that seems to sustain us must be laid down before we can experience real salvation. The scripture, "...take up his cross and follow Me..." has been misinterpreted for years to mean that every person will have some affliction in life that will be "their cross to bear." But it's not true. Taking up one's cross refers to giving up one's selfish existence. It refers to the sacrifice we make for the sake of God and the world, just like Jesus made. It means the same thing it meant to Jesus—'death to self'. We consecrate our life. We lose our life in order to save it.

However, notice that we must lose our life for His sake *and the gospel's sake*. Most Christians would say they have given their life for Jesus' sake, in that they acknowledge Him as their Lord and Savior. But the true Christian will also have given his life also for the *sake of the gospel*, which is the spreading of the good news and making disciples. It is not a command for full time ministers only. It is to *every* believer.

Even the actual Greek word for 'witness' ('martureo') reveals this principle. Martureo is where we get the English word 'martyr' from, which is used to describe those who die for their faith. Think about it. When Jesus said, "...and you shall be witnesses," He was actually labeling us as ones who have died—not physically, but given up our *selfishness* for Him.

> **From the time you get up in the morning till you go to bed at night, it's either Jesus or nothing. Either you have His love and compassion and His vision for the lost and dying, or you don't. Either you put Him first, or you put self first. If it's self first, then you're going to get messed up** (Hayes, p. 9).

What does it mean to lay down my life for the gospel's sake? It means that I must lay down my time, money, and comfort in order to spread the gospel of Jesus Christ. It takes faith to give our time to the work of God. It takes faith to give our money for the work of God. And it takes faith to give up our "I don't want to do anything that's uncomfortable" motto for the work of God. Our flesh doesn't usually want to step out of its comfort zone to share Christ with others. So, we must force it to obey us. Our flesh likes status quo. It doesn't like to be interrupted. Our flesh prefers to sit on the couch

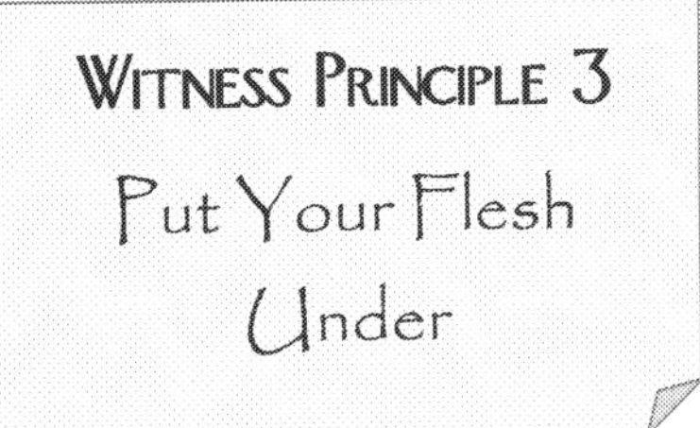

and not move. Our flesh would rather stay in bed where it's warm and comfortable. And our flesh would rather not take a chance on an uncomfortable conversation with a sinner. Our flesh would rather talk with friends at church than greet a new visitor or help encourage a new Christian. Our flesh would much rather go home for lunch with just the family than to invite a church visitor to lunch who has no Christian friends. But our spirit man wants something more.

After the giant of 'fear', we run into this second giant of 'not enough time for God'. We can easily be too busy and too concerned with our own daily tasks to make an effort to help someone else. That's called self-seeking. That's why Jesus requires us to "lose our life." It is very easy to stand in the grocery line and say nothing to anyone, not even the cashier. It is much harder to dig in your purse or pocket for a gospel tract or booklet and to bless someone with a kind gospel sentence. But, really, is it all that hard?

I arrived at the Tulsa airport one afternoon for a two week gospel campaign with Angelo Mitropoulos, and was standing at the conveyor waiting for my luggage. I noticed several business men standing together talking, also waiting for their luggage. And the thought crossed my mind that I should use this down time to share Christ with them. But here it came again, that same old—every Christian has it—spirit vs. flesh thought war, *Those guys are busy. I'm a stranger. They'll think I'm weird. Maybe this is weird. Will I get kicked out of the airport? Maybe they're already saved. Maybe they're not. Is it God? Is it not? You wimp. You know you should, but you can't, 'cause you're a wimp.* And blah, blah, blah, the internal conversation goes on, and I decide to just blow it off. But then I look outside to the street curb and notice that Angelo has arrived in his van with his two little girls to pick me up. I notice something else. His youngest daughter, five year old

Tina, is running up and down the sidewalk of the passenger pickup area handing gospel tracts to every person walking by. And that was it—iron sharpening iron. I couldn't let a five year old out-witness me, so I quickly got up the courage to pull my own tracts out of my jacket pocket, walked over to the group of businessmen, and spent 60 seconds handing out the Word of Eternal Life and sharing a brief, encouraging sentence or two about Jesus Christ. Ahhhh—what a great feeling of accomplishment. I, and five year old Tina, had just done our daily part for world evangelism (Evangelism—the practice of relaying information about a particular set of beliefs to others who do not hold those beliefs—the spreading of the good news).

Did it interrupt the group of men? Certainly. But the world needs to be interrupted. The lost are aimlessly drifting down the river of life, unaware of the waterfall of eternal death looming ahead. We, on the other hand, know what lies around the bend, and we are obligated to inform them, even if it means bothering their comfort zone on days other than Sunday. Do unsaved people want to be approached with something spiritual? Usually not. But unsaved people don't know what they don't know. God called Christians to intercept them and save them.

(Gospel tracts? Is this book going to be about street-corner-pamphlet-handing-out? No it is not. However, there is an important part that the printed Word of God plays in changing a life. And giving it to people is sometimes *the only way* to convey the clear gospel in a brief moment. Rather than my trying to defend the power of the written Word given to people, please just stay tuned, and all will be clear.)

4
Gone Fishing

Growing up, I was blessed to have parents who led me to Christ and taught me six solid, particular things that I knew were absolutes of God. The first was that the Bible is *the truth* and the final authority on everything. The second was that everyone needs to be born again through Jesus Christ. The third was that the baptism of the Holy Spirit (including tongues and power) is real and that everyone needs that. The fourth thing was that Christians don't have to be sick (I was instantly healed a couple times when Mom prayed, and then she taught me how to get healed and stay healed through the name of Jesus, which I learned by age 12.) The fifth thing I knew was that Christians are commanded to not be unequally yoked together with an unbeliever, which meant I couldn't marry someone who hadn't received Jesus as Lord and Savior. The sixth thing I knew was that all real Christians are to share their faith. And, I was around enough good Baptists to know that leading others to Jesus is part of the Christian life.

Personally, I drifted further and further away from the Lord for about ten years. But in my mid-twenties, I woke up and saw how far I was. I began to consider the Lord, went to church a couple of times, and began listening to a certain preacher explain the Word of God. It took me two months to assess my situation, count the cost of a life with God, and make a calculated decision to *follow* Jesus. I knew that coming fully into the kingdom of God meant sharing my faith. I knew that all my friends would have to know of my salvation and discipleship and that everyone in my path would have to know about Jesus. I might have been a rookie, but I had enough in me to know that surface Christianity had no place in a sincere walk with God and that sharing the gospel with others was a sincere matter. I thought I was way behind schedule. I thought I was going to have to catch up to all the great soul-winning witnesses for Christ. Turns out, there are a lot of Christians behind schedule. And we all need to catch up.

WITNESS PRINCIPLE 4

Fishing—It's What Christians Do

> **Then He said unto them, "Follow Me, and I will make you fishers of men"** (Matthew 4:19).

These were the first words Jesus said to any disciple. We've already examined His last words, which as it turns out, were a copy of these first words. He *commands* us to go after people. He wanted Peter and Andrew to do it, and He wants us to do it. All disciples, both then and now, are required to do it. One Bible paraphrase reads,

> **Join yourselves to me and be part of my mission, and you will pull people's lives out of meaninglessness and despair just as you are pulling fish from the sea** (Matthew 4:19).

Fishing for men—it's what Christians do.

We had a friend named Mary, who was a loving example of Jesus all her days, sharing Christ on a daily basis with whomever she met. Mary said that after she prayed to receive Jesus, the follow-up advice to her was this: that Friday night the church members were going out to share their faith, and that she would need to come. She didn't know any better, so she showed up and hit the streets to tell people about Jesus. The church members told her, "This is what Christians do." Mary just believed them, obeyed them, and went and crashed through the common fear and intimidation of sharing her faith, then got hooked on it. Fishing for men *really is* what Christians do. And we need to give ourselves to it until we are hooked on it. That's right. We need a holy addiction to this great call of leading others out of hell and into God's love.

Have you ever seen a sign or a plaque in a person's house with a fish or a fisherman on it and a caption that reads, "Gone Fishing"? We should be able to say that sometimes about ourselves. There should be frequent times when we step out of the natural course of life and share Christ with someone—out in the mall, on a vacation, at a birthday party, or at a restaurant. When those with us recognize what is happening, that we are once again letting our gospel commission interrupt our busy life, they can think to themselves, *they've gone fishing again.* If it's unsaved family members that see you, they might get perturbed or feel uncomfortable. But at least they'll know what real Christians do.

We do not have a choice; we are *commanded* to be fishers of men. The only choice we have in the matter is to follow Christ. Once you choose Him, Jesus said He will "*make* you fishers of men." It is the only time in Scripture that Jesus said He will *make* you do anything. If we are really following Christ, we will allow Him to *make* us win souls.

Notice He did not say "Follow Me, and I will show you a new religious custom." Nor did He say, "Follow Me, and I will show you how to be good on Sundays." No. Following Christ requires determined effort to keep up with Him. And Jesus is a soul-winner. Think of it this way: if Christ were in our shoes today, would He be doing what many do? Going to church, to school, to work, to the store, and back home, every day, ignoring sinners all day long? Definitely not. He would be helping people every chance He had, impacting every life that was in His path. Somehow, many Christians find it easy to *profess* Christ but hard to *follow* Christ. But not us; we are going to complete our Christian call of duty.

"Be ye therefore followers of God, as dear children" (Eph 5:1). The word 'followers' is a Greek word 'mimetes', which denotes a mimicker, or an imitator. We are to mimic Christ. Jesus said, "…as my Father hath sent Me, even so send I you" (John 20:21). Jesus was sent with a specific plan, a holy program to seek and save the lost, to heal the sick, to cast devils out of people, every day, everywhere He went. He was sent with authority from heaven. He was sent with power. He was sent to destroy the works of the devil and lead people out of darkness. He was the light of the world. So are you.

Where are the *world changers*? In the book of Acts, the world was being radically affected by the Christians, and it scared the religious heads. When Paul and Silas were arrested in Philippi, the magistrates said, "These men…exceedingly trouble our city." When Paul and Silas showed up in Thessalonica, the Jews said, "These who have turned the world upside down have come here too" (Acts 17:6). Many times, the apostles were told, "Do not speak or teach in this name (of Jesus) anymore." There was unholy resistance to heaven's good news.

Doesn't that make you want to rise up for the Lord? If we're going to rebel against something, why not rebel against what is *wrong*? Can't we recognize it's the devil that wants to stop the gospel? And shouldn't that make us want to join up, be a soldier, and bring this thing home? Where are the soldiers of the cross? Where are the world changers? Every real

Christian wants to do something big for God. And this is it. There's nothing bigger than bringing the next person to the saving knowledge of Jesus Christ. You might not get any money for it. And you might not get a plastic trophy or wall certificate for it. But there's still nothing bigger you can do for God.

5
The Witch Lady

"I am led by the Spirit, brother. I only talk to those He tells me to." I have heard this statement many times from people who don't approve of *every Christian* sharing the good news with *anyone and everyone.* Please understand that I believe we should all be led by the Spirit in helping others find Christ. Actually, we should all be led by the Spirit in all things (Romans 8:14). But there is also a line to draw. I don't have to be led by the Spirit to take a shower or brush my teeth every day, nor do I need to beg the Spirit to speak to me when to read my Bible, pray, or go to church. Those things are already an inherent part of my life. Likewise, I don't need to wait for the Spirit to prompt me to share the message of Jesus Christ. God allows us to make our own decisions for certain things, and He allows us to follow the written Word for other things without waiting for some spectacular leading of the Spirit.

If we get down to the truth, the Spirit has already given us a standing command through the mouth of Jesus, "Go ye into all the world and preach the gospel to *every creature...*" (Mark 16:15). By Bible commandment, we are required to preach to *everyone.* That is a pretty good leading of the Spirit, don't you think? It may not be very spectacular or hyper-spiritual, but it is still very supernatural. And if you simply decided to obey that one scripture the rest of your life without any extra leading of God, you'd stand before Jesus with honor and reward.

Waiting for perfect conditions is not acceptable. "He who observes the wind will not sow, And he who regards the clouds will not reap" (Ecclesiastes 11:4). Without taking initiative, there will always be some excuse in our way.

Here is a good way to look at it. It seems the Body of Christ has been sitting at the intersection at a red light, waiting for the Spirit to turn it green before approaching a sinner with the gospel. Let's turn it around: assume that the light is already green, and go for it unless the Spirit on some particular instance turns it red. He will do that occasionally, just like He did with Paul after He went through Galatia, "...they were forbidden by the Holy Spirit to preach the word in Asia." And again, "...they tried to go into Bithynia, but the Spirit did not permit them" (Acts 16:6-7). But it's okay to have a plan and start moving in a direction until He stops you. Further in the Book of Acts, we know that all of Asia heard the Word of God. So, it must have been a divine timing issue that delayed Paul. We need to be sensitive to the Spirit in allowing Him to alter our course sometimes, but we also need to be sensitive enough to get moving in the first place.

> **WITNESS PRINCIPLE 5**
>
> Turn Your Red Light Green

Notice Philip's early journey in the gospel, "Philip went down to the city of Samaria, and preached Christ unto them" (Acts 8:5). Notice he wasn't specifically led by the Spirit. The disciples had been scattered after the stoning of Stephen, and Philip probably just grabbed a couple of brothers and went to preach somewhere. The reason I don't think he was specifically led with a word from the Holy Spirit is that the scriptures do not say so. Whereas, further on in the same chapter, after revival breaks out and many are saved and healed, the scripture notes two specific leadings of God, "And *the angel of the Lord spake* unto Philip, saying, Arise, and go toward the south unto the way that goeth down from Jerusalem..." (Acts 8:26). "*Then the Spirit said* unto Philip, Go near, and join thyself to this chariot" (v. 29). Philip was not spoken to while at Jerusalem in his comfort zone, but only after he had put himself in a place of gospel service. If you'll start something by faith, you might be helped by an angel or a specific word from the Holy Spirit. But *you* must initiate *something*.

Here is an instance in my own life where I was initiated and started moving toward a plan, but then the Spirit interrupted me for something specific. At my first gospel assignment as a church member, I had volunteered to take a team of believers out to the community each Sunday afternoon to minister to people. We would take bread, cakes, and pastries out to various apartment complexes and call everyone out using a PA system that I hooked up to my pickup truck. I would announce, "Come down and get all the food you want, and if you're sick, come let us pray. Jesus will heal you right here on the street by the black pickup truck." We'd minister to the children and their parents, heal the sick, and lead people to the Lord. We continued this ministry for almost two years, and we saw many miracles of healing and many people saved. But one certain Sunday I discerned that the season was up. I didn't hear God say anything, but I knew in my heart that this apartment ministry was over for me, so I decided to end it. However, this particular week, I had already announced to the church that we would be going out again. So, in order to keep my word, I went ahead and showed up at 3:00 pm at the church to meet the others and head out. But no one else did. This was the first time in those two years that I was all alone for the outreach, but it didn't bother me since I already knew this was the last time. Again, though, I had already said I was going out that day, even if by myself. So I decided to pray a little extra before leaving the church. I wanted to pray and seek the Lord for a specific direction. I wanted Him to show me the exact apartment number in the exact complex. I wanted a vision, or a voice from heaven, or a ticker tape before my eyes of where to go. So I just prayed in the Spirit for about 30 minutes. And got nothing. I just kept praying until I felt like I was done. I felt empowered and ready to go, but I had not received any spectacular direction. No problem. You know, we don't usually get spectacular direction, especially when we're seeking it. We usually just get a slight spiritual sense about a thing.

So I drove off toward a certain apartment complex to which I had determined to go. Not too far down the road, I began to look left and right, just staying open to the Lord. And all of a sudden, only about a mile down the road, I found my head was locked to the left. I realized I was staring at a house, and my eyes didn't want to leave it. I noticed what I was looking at. It was a psychic fortune telling house with a big palm reader sign out front. I thought to the Lord, *There? You want me to go there? For what?* All I could envision was the Bible account of Paul casting the devil out of the fortune teller in Acts 16, and I only saw one car out front. So, I figured there was just one person in there—the witch, herself. I wondered to the Lord, *What would you have me do, cast the devil out of the witch lady?* I struggled within myself for a few seconds, and then I heard a voice from down in my spirit that gave me a warm electric feeling inside. God said, "Don't worry, just go." I obeyed. At the next light, I made a quick u-turn, drove to the house, and parked. As I walked up to the door, I noticed it was open, with only a screen door closed, and the lady inside saw me. As I walked up to the door, she asked, "Sir, would you like your fortune told?" I didn't say anything until I got all the way inside. Sitting at the table was the witch lady, and across from her were two young ladies, maybe nineteen or 20 years old. (I didn't realize it until later, but in the time it took me to make a u-turn, these two girls had driven in and parked. This is where our natural reasoning reveals its weakness. I had assumed there was only one person in the house.) I began to speak as a servant of God and make mention of Jesus Christ and Almighty God. As I did, two things happened. First, the witch lady began to sarcastically chime in as if she knew God, "Oh yes, we know, Jesus died for our sins…" which made me a bit mad. But also, one of the young ladies started expressing her embarrassment. She would look at me, and then put her head down, then look at her friend in disbelief, and then say "I can't believe this. Oh my, I can't believe this." I knew God was working on her, so I just kept talking a few more seconds until the witch lady got a little more forceful and pulled the ole', "Please, sir, this is my business. Can you please leave."

No problem. I had given the two ladies each a gospel tract, and as I walked out, I said, "Ladies, you know this isn't right, so make the right choice." And I went to my truck and drove off. I felt really good about it. I knew God had led me specifically and used me to help someone. I was tearing up a bit as I prayed and thanked God. And I began to pray, "Lord, have mercy on those girls and get those girls out of there." But all of a sudden, God interrupted me. That same voice spoke up from within me, and with more force than previously, said, "You get them out of there!" Well, I had only driven up as far as that same street light, so I made the same u-turn, drove to the house and parked again. As I walked up, the fortune teller saw me coming and said through the screen door, "Sir, I told you. Please. This is my business." I stopped where I was, about 20 feet from the door, and yelled firmly, "Ladies, God said get out NOW!" Those two girls popped up out of their chairs like lightning had hit them and came running outside!

I walked them to their cars and found out why the one girl seemed so startled. She said, "I just can't believe this. I have been trying to get my fortune told for three months, and something always happens to stop me. The last time my boyfriend's car...and now this! How many times have you done this to get people out of there?" I said, "None, this was my only time. God sent me here."

She explained that she had received Jesus as Lord and Savior only a year prior, but that she hadn't been going to church. She had a feeling that it was wrong to see the fortune teller, but no one had told her for sure. I prayed with the girls and rejoiced with them that God cared for and loved them, and wanted to help them have a better future without a demonized person's help. We parted. And I headed to that apartment complex, put gospel tracts on every door, and went home. Glory to God. Not very long after that, the psychic house closed up and was sold.

How did this happen? It happened because I had made a move. I started off to do something for God, and then in the process, He led me more specifically. Notice that God wouldn't do it without me. He wanted one of His servants to do something in the natural realm to save the girls from the devilish influence. If you want to do something supernatural, if you want some holy excitement in life, you can't lounge around on your couch waiting for God to speak to you. It won't happen that way. A docked boat cannot be steered. And a believer sitting at a red light, planning on doing nothing, cannot be directed by God and will miss out on some real, holy fun.

6
You're Already There

We pastors sometimes feel stuck trying to get church members unlocked from the church building and out to the community to touch people. But really, church members aren't locked in the building. They're only in the building about two to six hours a week. The rest of the time, guess where they are? They're out. They're out in the community—the marketplace, the schools, businesses, and neighborhoods—the whole world around them.

You don't need to wait for the special outreach to impact your community, because you're already *in* the community—every week, every day, as soon as you leave the church building, you're there. So awake to the world all around you and impact it. Be instant in season and out of season. This is lifestyle Christianity. What is the pastor's role? It is to edify and remind the saints while they're in, so they can be more effective while they're out.

After giving the disciples "authority against unclean spirits, to cast them out, and to heal all manner of sickness and all manner of disease," Jesus said, "And *as you go*, preach, saying the kingdom of heaven is at hand, heal the sick, cleanse the lepers, raise the dead, cast out devils..." (Matthew 10:7-8).

This gives us a strategy. *As we go,* we can be on the lookout for people to help. As we go to work, as we go to school, as we go to eat, as we live our lives, we can preach, heal, and cast out. Jesus did it. If you just examine the two chapters prior to Jesus telling them, *as you go...*, we see Jesus' lifestyle of helping people. He didn't wait for the sanctuary. He didn't reserve His goodness for the synagogue or formal meeting. He was always open to helping needy people. Walking down from a mountain, He allowed the leper to interrupt him. He healed him. Next, he entered a city, and a centurion interrupted him to heal a servant. He did. Next, Jesus enters into Peter's house and finds the mother-in-law sick with fever. He healed her. Then He goes on a boat ride, only to encounter a demon possessed man on the other side. He freed him. And so on.

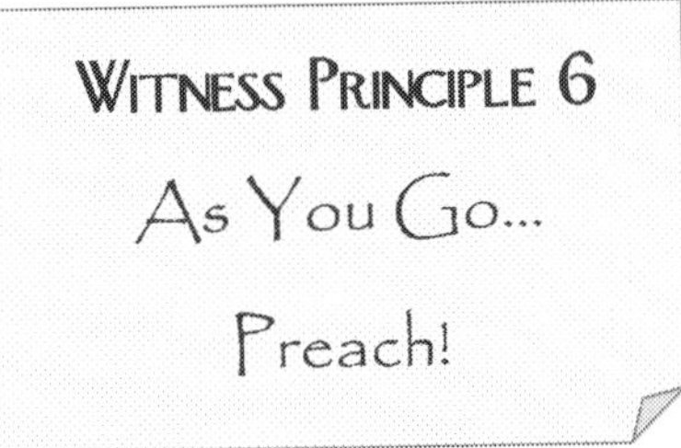

You get the picture. To be like Jesus, we will need to allow life's interruptions with other people to be our opportunity to serve God and fulfill our call. The word 'Christian' is literally translated 'little Christ'. It was what non-believers called believers. Why? Because they were talking and acting like Jesus, turning the world upside down right out in public.

My first exploit as a new, re-committed Christian was not in a church. It was in a restaurant parking lot. At the time, even though I was Spirit-filled, I was attending a Baptist church, and I was spending a lot of time with the singles group of the church. About 20 of us had gone out to eat dinner at a restaurant. Upon leaving, we all headed to our own cars with a plan to re-gather at someone's apartment, and I was about to start my truck when I heard a frantic knock on my window. One of the group had come to get me because one of our friends had fallen to the ground having an epileptic seizure. Instantly my mind went to the Bible account of Jesus healing the demon possessed boy who was torn with a seizure, and I thought *that's a demon, and I am going to cast it out.* I casually walked across the parking lot to the crowd of my friends who were gathered around watching the seizure. (I say casually, because I didn't walk fast. But inside me, I was excited and nervous, as I had recently been filled with the Holy Spirit and power, and this was the first big thing to need that power. I knew I was on the hook.) As I approached, the crowd parted for me and I leaned over to verify that our friend was in a full blown seizure. It appeared so, as her eyes were rolled back, her tongue was out, and she was shaking all over. Right in front of everybody, I quickly placed my hand on her stomach and shouted, "Satan, I command you to come out of her in the name of Jesus!" Immediately, her eyes opened, she stopped shaking, and the seizure ended. I was glad about that. Everyone was—all the Baptists. We all started praising God, some out of joy, some out of panic, and some out of "what just happened here?" About that time a fire truck and paramedic arrived, but she was already back to normal. The rest of the story is that for a while at that Baptist church, I was the go-to person for healing and demon-casting-out, and we saw some mighty miracles happen to people. But eventually, the news made it up the ranks, and the pastors informed me that I was no longer allowed to pray for the sick. (But that's okay. I was prepared, since Jesus told us the servant is not greater than his Master—if they didn't approve of Him, they wouldn't approve of us.) So, I did what Jesus did, and went elsewhere. For the friend who had been plagued with seizures all her life, a couple of us Spirit-filled "baby" Christians ministered to her one more time after that. One year later, she contacted me and informed me that she had one slight seizure about a month after, but for the rest of the year, and for the first time in her life, she was totally healed. Praise the Lord.

Christian ministry in the community—the story continues. That night, we all finally made it to the apartment to hang out and fellowship. And while we were sitting around, another of our friends jumps up, grabs her chest in pain, and runs outside. I thought, *well, I can and should help.* So, I followed her and her friend outside. She had a heart condition and was having a severe attack of some sorts. I offered to pray for her and she agreed. This was only the second person I had ever prayed for (the first was an hour prior in the parking lot). So, I really didn't know what to do. I put my hand on her head and prayed that God would heal her in Jesus' name. Immediately, she calmed down and felt fine, 'ooh-ing' and 'ahh-ing' that some warm feeling came all over her from her head down. And she was healed. Several months later, I asked about her heart condition, and she realized that she hadn't had any more symptoms at all.

My point is that spreading the gospel, healing the sick, and casting out devils should be part of our lifestyle. So, rather than wait for a mission trip or for the weekend outreach, we should expect to distribute the Word and the power to people *as we go, anytime* we go, and *everywhere* we go. I assure you, it makes every day a lot more interesting and a lot more fruitful.

John G. Lake said of Matthew 10:8 ("...heal the sick, cast out devils, raise the dead...") that this is a *strong man's gospel.* He said,

> Christianity was not to be stinted in her giving. She was not to be a beggar. She was to be a giver. She had something from heaven to give that the world did not have. She had something to give that would bring deliverance to the world. Jesus was putting His program of deliver-

ance in force through the Church. The man is a bold man who undertakes to carry out this program of Jesus. The Christian who never has faith enough in God to undertake it, I fear, is of the cowardly type. I am afraid that modern Christianity stands indicted at the bar of God for cowardliness because of fear to undertake the program of Jesus (Lake, p. 529).

7
Unashamed

I am not ashamed of the gospel of Christ: for it is the power of God to salvation to everyone who believes... (Romans 1:16).

Here comes the 'gut check' where we judge our own selves. Am I *ever* ashamed of the gospel? Am I ever embarrassed to talk of my own salvation or of the truth of the Bible? Am I ever afraid of being misunderstood or laughed at? If so, then I must be honest—I am ashamed. Maybe not in general, deep down in my heart—I mean, I believe in the Lord, and I'll never turn from Him. But on the outside, I'm more concerned how others might view me than of what God needs of me. But don't be discouraged. Most all of us had that weakness at some point in the beginning. But this life of faith does not allow us to just accept our weakness and give up. Instead, we're obligated by Jesus' precious blood to get strong, obey God unashamedly, and be willing to lose our "reputation."

I learned a different attitude about it. I decided that this kingdom of God is more real than the kingdom of the world, and that I have something that no one can live without. Because Jesus lives in me, I have the answer to every single problem of life. I know exactly what it takes to make someone's life complete. They *must* listen to me. They can't live one more day without my God. They can't afford to go to hell. There is no way for me to be ashamed. I have been saved by my Lord. I am a new man, full of the Spirit of a holy God, and He is counting on me to tell the truth.

To never be ashamed, the Christian is required to think spiritually. The gospel is not a natural conversation piece. It is supernatural in nature. Paul said of the gospel "…it is the power of God." What we share with people is seemingly foolish to the worldly person, but nonetheless it is all powerful. If you bought a fine new car, would you be ashamed to tell people? If you just moved into a brand new home, would there be any hesitation to share that good news that blessed you so? It should be the same, and more so, with the salvation of God. If you are convinced that Jesus Christ is the answer to life, and eternal life, then you can overcome all shame of sharing Him with others.

For me, it has helped knowing where I sit in the scheme of things. I am seated with Christ, on the throne of God, "God…has made us sit together in the heavenly places in Christ Jesus" (Ephesians 2:6). And from way up here, there is nothing to be embarrassed about. The whole earth has been eagerly anticipating the "manifestation of the sons of God." *And we're it.* We are the sons of God who are entrusted with spreading this gospel. Therefore, this Christian life means never apologizing for the truth of God's Word.

WITNESS PRINCIPLE 7

Never Be Ashamed

Always be ready to give a defense to everyone who asks you a reason for the hope that is in you, with meekness and fear (1 Peter 3:15).

I allowed the Lord to stretch my comfort zone by acting on various impromptu impulses (some His, some mine), even if they were scary. One time in a post office lobby, I got everyone's attention (those who were stuck in line with me) and preached to them a short message of Jesus Christ, then handed them all a gospel tract. Another time after driving a lady to the doctor's office, I was sitting in the waiting room looking at the built-in book shelves they had for decoration. I noticed an old Bible sitting in the shelf. So, I picked it up, opened it to a healing scripture, and stood up to preach to the three or four patients who were waiting in the room. I shared a message and offered to pray for anyone to be healed. No one responded, so I sat down and went about my business. One time on an airplane I had been seated near the front. After we landed, I stood and faced all those who were exiting. And as they walked by, I greeted them as if I worked for the airline, "Have a nice day. Thank you for flying." And I handed everyone a gospel tract. If their hands were full, I shoved it into their carry-on luggage pockets as I bid them farewell. One time in New York, I took a subway trip just so I could force myself to preach to people. Right in the middle of the packed subway car, I shouted for everyone to listen as I preached a short message and handed them all gospel tracts. Not all of my spontaneous ideas produce visible results, but I know the seed of God's Word is just as important. And many of the things are equally important for my own freedom—to keep me unashamed of the Lord and His Words.

> **WITNESS PRINCIPLE 8**
>
> It's All Clear on Judgment Day

Whosoever therefore shall be ashamed of me and of my words in this *adulterous and sinful generation*; of him also

shall the Son of man be ashamed, when he cometh in the glory of his Father with the holy angels (Mark 8:38).

Think about it. One day, we'll all stand in eternity. We'll all be judged, "...some to everlasting life, and some to shame and everlasting contempt" (Dan 12:2). In that day, all the evildoers will see the ugliness and shame of their sin. The righteous will be glorified and honored. Though the wicked may laugh and scoff now while they live in the deceiving pleasure of a godless life, their glorying is only for a few years. Our victory will last for eternity.

When we get a picture of the beauty of holiness and the stench of sin, we'll no longer have any shame to speak the truth in love. In the middle of this society that is openly defying God and despising all that is good, where the rule of thumb is pleasure above all else, where fornication is the underlying goal of almost every thought and motive and advertisement, and open rebellion against authority is perpetuated in television shows that reach multitudes and basically train the children of the world, is there any way for us to keep quiet? Even if we consider "good people" who refuse to acknowledge the Word of God, we realize they are in *total rebellion* against the Lord. If we remain silent, the poor, blinded heathen only have one choice—to remain in their destructions.

The ungodly world is the one that should be ashamed of its life—not us. They are the ones who are in danger of judgment. When we shine, the Spirit informs sinners that they are wrong and without God. But when we are inactive in our witness, the Holy Spirit does not move to convince them of their sin.

Do not be afraid of the pitiful, sinful world. It is in desperate need of righteousness, and you have the answer. There is absolutely no reason to ever be ashamed of God's holiness or His Word. Judgment day is coming, and it will all be clear.

> **And they that be wise shall shine as the brightness of the firmament; and they that turn many to righteousness as the stars forever and ever** (Daniel 12:3).

Let me inspire you with this great declaration,

> I am a part of the fellowship of the Unashamed. I have the Holy Spirit Power. The die has been cast. I have stepped over the line. The decision has been made. I am a disciple of Jesus Christ. I won't look back, let up, slow down, back away, or be still. My past is redeemed, my present makes sense, and my future is secure. I am finished and done with low living, sight walking, small planning, smooth knees, colorless dreams, tame visions, mundane talking, chintzy giving, and dwarfed goals.
>
> I no longer need preeminence, prosperity, position, promotions, plaudits, or popularity. I don't have to be right, first, tops, recognized, praised, regarded, or rewarded. I now live by presence, learn by faith, love by patience, lift by prayer, and labor by power.
>
> My pace is set, my gait is fast, my goal is Heaven, my road is narrow, my way is rough, my companions few, my Guide is reliable, my mission is clear. I cannot be bought, compromised, deterred, lured away, turned back, diluted, or delayed. I will not flinch in the face of sacrifice, hesitate in the presence of adversity, negotiate at the table of the enemy, ponder at the pool of popularity, or meander in the maze of mediocrity.
>
> I won't give up, back up, let up, or shut up until I've preached up, prayed up, paid up, stored up, and stayed up for the cause of Christ. I am a disciple of Jesus Christ. I must go until He returns, give until I drop, preach until all know, and work until He comes.
>
> And when He comes to get His own, He will have no

problem recognizing me. My colors will be clear for "I am not ashamed of the Gospel, because it is the power of God for the salvation of everyone who believes" (Romans 1:16) (Dr. Bob Moorehead).

8
I'm So Glad You're Here!

While the earth remains, seedtime and harvest, and cold and heat, and summer and winter, and day and night, shall not cease (Genesis 8:22).

If we'll keep in mind that salvation of the soul is like seedtime and harvest, it will be much easier on us. The physical law of harvest requires that a seed is first planted. We can't only pray harder. If the farmers of the world decided not to plant any seed one year but instead to just pray for a miracle harvest, we would all laugh at them. Actually, our laughing would turn to crying the next year because we wouldn't have any corn on the cob or peanuts at the ball park.

In the same way, the world is starving for the Word of God because of a lack of seed planting. The spiritual law of harvest requires that seed is first planted, because the harvest is *inside that seed.* If the seed doesn't go into the ground, nothing will spring up from which to pluck fruit. Of course, the seed is the Word of God, and the believers (not just the pulpit preachers, and not just the television preachers) are the farmers. Praying for the lost may help the seed grow, but praying alone can do nothing without seed planting.

Seedtime

Seedtime is extremely easy; every believer can do it. To plant a vegetable seed in a garden, all it takes is a few seconds to drop a seed into a hole and cover it up. Planting the Word into the world is just as easy: walk in love toward everybody, perform frequent deeds of kindness, distribute gospel books, literature, and media, post your church's best sermon videos onto Facebook, and tell *everyone* how to be saved and healed. And don't necessarily require any response from anybody (when a farmer plants seed in the ground, he doesn't expect it to produce fruit the very next day—he allows the *seed* to take its *time).*

WITNESS PRINCIPLE 9

Seedtime and Harvest, Just Like a Farmer

> **Listen! Behold, there went out a sower to sow…as he sowed, some fell by the way side…some fell on stony ground, some fell among thorns, and some fell on good ground…** (Mark 4:1-8).

What kind of farmer is this? Why isn't he watching what he's doing? I mean, he's wasting his seed. He seems careless. No. He's fine. We know the seed is the Word of God and this farmer is the believer. This parable shows us not only the different types of people who hear the Word but also a spiritual principle concerning *how to plant your seed.*

Plant it everywhere. Be liberal with this good news. Don't pick and choose where to plant it. Just "shout it from the rooftops" so to speak. You've got plenty of seeds of: love, joy, kindness, gospel tracts, emails, Twitter messages—words of life in every form. According to the parable, many seeds may not make it. They will die. But that is not your business. Your business is to plant and water, and let God do the growing.

One teenager at our church sent a text message to all of his friends, giving a brief message about Jesus wanting to save their soul. He instructed them to text him back if they wanted to be saved, and five friends responded, "Yes." He led all five of them to confess Christ—all through his phone! (Of course, we realize that making disciples includes more than a one-time confession. But we've first got to get people through the Door so they can have the deposit of the Holy Spirit and a chance to go on.)

Witnessing success is not determined by how many you harvest. Success is only determined by your being an active farmer. *How many people believe you* is not what determines your heavenly treasure. It's how consistent and faithful you were. Recognize that Jesus preached and blessed thousands of people, but at the end, there were only 120 believers in the upper room. Remember that even the great ministry of Paul the Apostle included moments of very small numbers. When the Lord sent him to Macedonia, he led only one woman to the Lord before he and Silas were arrested, beaten, and thrown in prison for casting a devil out of a lady. Sitting in prison, Paul and Silas were completely successful because they had done the will of God. Numbers don't tell the full story, so don't rely on them as your sole success indicator.

Harvest

Harvest is also extremely easy also; every believer can do it. When I once planted my annual tomato garden, I planted seed in every spot possible. However, when I reaped the harvest, I only picked the tomatoes that had started ripening and changing color. It is more important to be led by the Spirit when reaping the harvest than it is when planting seed. Attempting to pick green tomatoes is much more difficult and will take force. But red, or ripening, tomatoes basically fall into your hand. Tell every sinner about Jesus, but look for the ripe, ready one before challenging them to go further and receive Christ. The sinner who is ready to be saved will be easily recognizable. Their openness will be apparent. They might be asking you what they asked Peter in Acts Chapter 2, "What shall we do?" Or, "Can I come to church with you?" Or, "Please tell me how I can have such joy and peace as you do." Just tell them to call on the Lord Jesus, and they'll be saved (Romans 10:13). And if you are not sure if they believe or if they want to be saved, you can always ask.

One reason that being a witness seems so scary is that we've had a tough time picking green tomatoes. Green tomatoes want to argue. They don't want to get in your basket. So leave them alone. "Green" sinners just need more truth to believe and more time to "ripen on the vine." Don't try to force them. Don't ever argue God with people.

Back to the term *fishers of men*—if you've ever fished for fish, you're aware that catching them requires some finesse. Have you ever seen someone go jumping and yelling and splashing into the water to grab a fish? Probably not. Instead, we carefully choose our bait and then we expertly cast the hook. Then we wait. In order to hook that fish and reel it in, it must first take the bait. So it is with the sinner. Be patient. See if they take your bait before you try to catch them (see if they believe what you are saying). If they don't bite, throw another bait. If they still don't bite, then don't do anything. Yanking the hook is useless if they haven't taken the bait. Maybe you can get them next time.

What kind of bait am I talking about? Truth. Godly wisdom. Love. And questions. Learn to ask people questions to find out what they believe. One to one witnessing is all about conversation. Let people talk, and look for a way to ask leading questions that lead them to a decision for Christ. Later in the book, we'll go through some of these details.

There was a certain cashier at the haircut salon that I talked with about the Lord. She was very interested for a couple months, and I could tell she was seriously considering coming to Christ and even coming to church. But then, all of a sudden, she turned cold. I realized that it was no use trying to speak anymore about the Lord, so I just decided to be nice and joyful to her each time I came. I did that for one and a half years. I could tell that she was a bit convicted during that time, but I still felt that I couldn't speak to her. Until one day. One day I walked into the salon and she came running up to me with quiet desperation and said, "I'm so glad you're here. I need God in my life." (Now that's an easy catch.) She went on to describe how she had been in a relationship with a guy for one and a half years, was ready to get out of it, and realized where her life needed to go. I told her that after my haircut, I would find her and help her. I did, and she told her manager she was taking a break. We went out into the mall, and she prayed to receive Christ right in the middle of all the shoppers. On my next visit about a month later, she was a changed woman. She noticed that her lifestyle was changing and that she no longer wanted to do the same things as her friends. She had even begun trying to persuade her people to change and turn to God. Praise the Lord.

What happened? The seed had been planted and grown, and she had "ripened" and was ready. All I did was show up.

9
What Is My Ministry?

It's like people have fallen overboard and are drowning in the water, and no one is throwing them a rope. Those on the boat are confusedly self-reflecting on their personal titles, "I don't know if I'm a teacher or a helps ministry." "I'm not sure if I'm a mercy gift, or an exhorter." "Well, I know one thing for sure, I've got the ministry of giving…and my wife, well she's definitely a so-n-so."

Wait a second. Can someone throw the rope?

"But, I have this special gift to do great things, and I think God may be calling me to xyz…"

Hello? Please throw the rope.

I don't really care what you are right now. Maybe just start functioning—start doing something, and we'll decide what to call you later. For now, can someone just throw the rope? Can we just please pause our little personal ministry campaigns and throw the rope to the dying people? Yes, the rope with the little donut floaty thing on it—just toss that into the water please before the drowning people go under. Can we muster up enough focus for that? I'm a this, I'm a that, he's a this, she's a that. Well, I'm not sure what I am. But can we all please just start throwing some ropes!

"But I don't know if I've been trained properly on throwing the rope. What if I don't throw it perfectly?" Again...please...just throw the rope. The more times you throw it, the better you'll get at it. But right now, *people are suffering and headed to hell.*

It's like a basketball team arguing up and down the court over who should shoot the ball into the basket. "I don't care, just someone shoot the ball, would you!" When we lose sight of the goal, we get distracted. All the strife and nonsense and all the ridiculous newfangled teaching that goes on in churches is because folks forget our commission. Like a parent who addresses a room full of chaotic, bantering children, "If you kids don't find something productive to do and stop your bickering, I'll find something for you." It's the same with the Church.

It's like a town is flooding and all residents are called to pile sandbags to save the city. Someone runs over to the doctor's office to recruit him, but he is too busy doing his doctor stuff, "But I'm a doctor. I need not stoop so low as to lug sand bags around." Then the lawyer, then the preacher—they are too busy doing their more important things. Could you guys please just pile some sand bags? All doctors, all lawyers, all preachers....the town is flooding! We'll give you some special applause for your important work and sort everything out after we get to heaven, but for now, can you just help save the city? If you don't, your Christianity becomes confusing to others because—remember?—it's what Christians do.

Christians have long-labored in the uncertainty about "what is *my* ministry, Lord? What am *I* called to do?" And there is little need for that. If you listen closely, there is usually a tone of *self* in the pursuit of one's call. Don't fall into the trap of needing some unique ministry to help you feel special. You already *are* special. And leading people to Jesus is *supremely* special. What is your call? I have your answer. I can tell you exactly what your ministry is. I don't even need a prophetic word about it. All I need is the Bible. It seems that many have esteemed personal prophetic words, visions, and special callings more highly than the Bible, but it should not be. Especially if we want to be solid, stable Christians, we're going to have to position ourselves first on the written Word of God. And the Word is clear about it. We are called to *the ministry of reconciliation.*

> **WITNESS PRINCIPLE 10**
>
> Here's Your Ministry:
>
> The Ministry of Reconciliation

> **Now all things are of God, who has reconciled us to Himself through Jesus Christ, and has *given us the ministry of reconciliation* (not some of us, but all of us), that is, that God was in Christ reconciling the world to Himself, not imputing their trespasses to them, and has committed to us the word of reconciliation. Now then, we are ambassadors for Christ** (2 Corinthians 5:18-20).

Both as the Church, and also as individuals, God has given us this 'ministry of reconciliation'. I have a ministry. You have a ministry. And it is that. Reconcile means *to restore to friendship or harmony, to settle the differences between two parties.* And God needs us to do our ministry—to settle the differences between God and people. We are to help people meet God through Jesus Christ and grow thereby. We have been sent by the Lord to do so: *we are ambassadors for Christ.* An ambassador is *an authorized representative or messenger sent to do business on behalf of the one who sent him in the land to where he is sent.* The people of God are on this earth to do heaven's business.

What I have seen is that until the believer does what the Bible says about being a witness, they never fully succeed in any other specific ministry arena. Or, maybe they have some success as a teacher or preacher, but not as a Christian (you know, teachers and preachers have a two-fold judgment—one, as a Christian, and two, as a five-fold minister), and they may never have true contentment in the gospel because of neglecting their first Christian call of duty. It is very possible to be distracted by all the "more important ministry things" and self-absorbed with promoting one's ministry to the point that personal witnessing is not only forgotten, but even looked down upon. I have a feeling there are preachers who have this attitude and end up going years without sharing their faith with anyone outside the pulpit.

Some might think *but I'm a pastor, I don't really need to deal with outside people.* Wait a second. Jesus was the greatest Pastor of all, and yet first, He was a soul-winner. *But I'm an apostle. I'm much too valuable to the Church to spend time witnessing to the common sinner.* Jesus was the first and greatest Apostle, and yet He was a soul-winner. *I'm a famous evangelist. If I can't preach to thousands, I'm not wasting my time.* Again, need I say it? Jesus was the greatest Evangelist of all, and yet He took time to talk to one woman at the well, one man in a tree, or one maniac on the shore. The same goes for a *teacher* and a *prophet.* Jesus was both, and still cared for the lone person. Your calling to the Body of Christ in no way negates your individual responsibility as a Christian—to be a witness in your world. Some have said, "You get them saved, and I will teach and disciple them." Nope. You do both. Others have said, "My ministry is as a prophet in the Church.

You know, prophesying to people is what I do." Nope. Be careful not to miss your Christian call, for if you are truly a prophet, you will be judged twice: both as prophet and also as Christian. (And by the way, prophesying to people doesn't make one a prophet. There are several other essential attributes of a true prophet in the Church.)

> **"God had no children too weak, but a great many too strong to make use of."**
>
> —D. L. Moody

> **"If you preachers would start winning souls everywhere you go, you wouldn't have to get a book of illustrations to preach from next Sunday."**
>
> —Jack Hyles

Likewise, I've seen believers feel personally special for being a faithful viewer and monthly partner of the famous television preacher with all the elaborate new teachings, while they completely ignore the soul-winning and kingdom building efforts of their own church going on right in front of them. Why? Because they never accepted the high calling of God of sharing their faith and helping to make disciples. Somehow, it seems more appealing to just *attend* something famous than to *do* something so routine and un-applauded.

Heaven applauds it, though.

Though many will get specific direction from God at times, and though all have a specific function within the Body of Christ, we are all called to the same basic ministry. We all have the same call. The entire Body of Christ is called to work toward the same end. It is to bring God to people. Not realizing this, and not majoring on it, is the reason so many Christians are so far from sharing their faith with others. We have elevated the glamorous gifts and spectacular ministries so much that it's created a wide disparity in the minds of believers. They feel there's no way to be as equipped and as effective as the "great" ones, so why try? I'll tell you why. Because the "big preachers" can't go where you go. They don't have access to the people you have access to. You are right where God has positioned you, with people who need God, and it's time to erase all excuses and participate in this ministry.

We have a ministry. We have a job. We have a holy purpose on this earth. That purpose is to spread our personal salvation to others. We don't want to go to heaven alone. We want to bring many with us. And we only have one earth life to fulfill that purpose. Like Jesus said, we've got to work while it is day. The night comes, when no man can work. I've noticed that many Christians are failing in life because they've lost their purpose. They're too distracted by the world, by cares, by self interests, by financial problems and family crises, and they have a hard time keeping victory in anything. And it's all because they have no spiritual purpose. Then they start searching for spiritual purpose, trying to find a role or a project that will seem fulfilling enough. But it never does because they've skipped Project One: the ministry of reconciling sinners to Christ.

Let me mention a man of God you should know of, T.L. Osborn. He is really the modern day Church's pioneer of the overseas mass evangelistic crusade, where he gathered historical crowds and won millions to Christ in approximately 76 countries during the mid to late 1900's. He and his wife were not just platform preachers, but they were personal soul-winners who committed their lives to the one as well as to the multitude. I heard brother Osborn say at a conference one time about all the "special callings" everyone seems to want, "I don't know what I am. I didn't get one of those calls. I'm just a believer. I didn't get the call to a country, so we just got the map of the world out and drew a circle around the whole thing. I didn't feel anything. I guess I'm just a dud when it comes to feeling. If I missed it and went to the wrong country or something, I guess Jesus will just correct me in heaven."

You are called. You have a ministry. Do this first.

"The monument I want after I am dead is a monument with two legs going around the world—a saved sinner telling about the salvation of Jesus Christ."
—D.L. Moody

Our Secondary Callings

Now that we've prioritized things and established some right perspective, we can acknowledge exclusive individual callings and positions in the Body of Christ. Another book could be written on this subject, because the Christian should want to please the Lord in every way. The Lord Jesus will place you in the Body as it *pleases Him*. He may call you to do a grand thing or a small thing, a visible thing or a hidden thing. He may use you more in the public view or in private. Your unique callings are just as important to the Lord as your Scriptural callings, but they come second. We should value our unique callings and gifts of God that He has placed on us, but not overvalue them to the point of self-worth. Our worth should be tied up in the person of Christ, where we are of extreme value and where any gift of God upon us is only our duty to others and not a means of self-indulgence. We must take heed not to allow our unique gifts and callings to deceive us into a place of too much self-gratification and glory seeking. Many have a problem doing things for the Lord because of the "what's in it for me?" reasoning. I've watched many people stuck in limbo saying, "I just want to be used by God..." that they've become utterly *useless* to God. They are too self-focused, looking too far out into the future, searching for something of significance and recognition. And they neglect the good things in front of them, becoming almost completely useless for current good works. Others have been deceived by the worldly quest for doing something *that's very rewarding and fulfilling*. I've had people tell me since I left my career for full time ministry, "Well, I'm glad you're doing something that's probably so rewarding to you." It sounds so feeble when they say that, because that has nothing to do with it. It's not about me, and that's not why I do it. It's all about God. Fulfilling the plan and purpose of God will far surpass the common feelings of self substantiation. And until we get to the bottom of 'self' like Paul did, we'll never be content in this life.

> **"I am crucified with Christ: nevertheless I live; yet not I, but Christ lives in me: and the life which I now live in the flesh I live by the faith of the Son of God, who loved me, and gave himself for me"** (Galatians 2:20).

Here is a brief summary on fulfilling your purpose in the Lord. First, start functioning now, right where you are. If you can't be great in your current place, God sees no benefit in giving you the next. Be sure that you are consecrated fully to God and His kingdom. If you never *lose your life*, on purpose, for His sake and the gospel, you'll be on your own without the grace of God. Know the will of God, and use your faith to get there. Get a vision in your heart and cultivate it. But remember, your vision is not just some great future accomplishment. Vision includes the journey. Your vision for life must include a place for you to live and succeed *now—today*. If not, you'll never feel content. And your vision does not have to be something of your own. It can be the vision of another that you support until Jesus comes. In the kingdom of God, everyone doesn't have to build his own separate thing. Be faithful now with what you are doing and to whom you are with. Trust God and His grace, and be patient for the day things change.

Don't you believe God is big enough to not let you fail or miss it? Promotion cometh from above, so know that it's all God anyway—no human manipulation is needed for you to achieve your high calling of God. Let God be the decision Maker, for He does know best. Don't compare yourself to others. Comparisons are dangerous. Keep your eye on the finish line of pleasing God. And pray in tongues—a lot. Praying in tongues is your secret weapon of speaking mysteries and paving the way for your future to come to pass. And remember, this is a journey, and it matters *how* you travel. So be a loving witness of Jesus Christ along the way.

10
What If God's Perfect Will Is *You*?

Whoever calls on the name of the Lord shall be saved. How then shall they call on Him in whom they have not believed? And how shall they believe in Him of whom they have not heard? And *how shall they hear without a preacher*? (or without a believer like you?) (Romans 10:13-14).

I once knew a certain Christian man who attended my home church men's weekly prayer meeting. One morning, he shared with the group how a friend of his had died. He said that the friend had been part of his car pool group for many years in Houston, and that he had a sudden heart attack and died. I asked if his friend was saved, and his answer startled me. He said, "I don't know. I never talked to him about that." Nothing else was said about it, and we moved on in our prayer meeting. But I instantly realized what a tragedy this might have been. All those years, all those hours in the car together, all those words that were probably spoken to one another, and not one mention of Jesus or one question of the friend's spiritual belief? What if this car pool season was the final, God-ordained opportunity for this friend to hear the gospel? What if this man was his friend's last real chance to receive Jesus? And the Christian neglected his duty. I know some might be saying, "Wait, you can't judge him, what if God didn't want him to share Christ with the man?" Okay, well, my point is not to condemn the brother. There's no need for that. But I'm sure that we've already proved God's will—that He absolutely *did* want him to share Christ with his friend.

> **"How shall I feel at the judgment if multitudes of missed opportunities pass before me in full review, and all my excuses turn out to be nothing more than displays of my cowardice and fear."**
>
> —Jonathan Edwards

I once had a certain haircutter that I began going to for about six months (I like to rotate haircutters fairly often so that I can offer salvation to them all. I've decided that their eternity is more important than my perfect, consistent haircut.) His name was Peter, and he was a self-proclaimed atheist. His wife had recently been saved and Spirit-filled, and he had spent careful time resisting her as best he could. Each time I sat in his chair, I looked for opportunity to share something with him about God. And each time, he reluctantly but kindly listened. As time went on, he began to take my bait and ask questions, and then he would allow me to answer them. Eventually, I bought him a Bible, and he began reading the New Testament (always remind people to begin there, rather than the Old Testament). I never personally prayed with him to receive Jesus. But one day, he tells me that something must have happened

> **WITNESS PRINCIPLE 11**
>
> How Can They Hear Without *You?*

to him because at a family gathering, he found himself arguing the case for Christ with his parents and explaining why Jesus is the only way. He had been born again. The last time I saw him, He was reading his namesake books—1st and 2nd Peter.

And then he died. He had a sudden heart attack one morning and died before he was 40. But he died saved. Barely. I don't think he ever made it to church with his wife, but she knew something spiritual had happened to him and that I was involved. And several co-workers had confirmed to her of Peter's conversion. She asked me to preach at his funeral, where I gladly accepted and explained to hundreds of his friends what had happened to him spiritually, how God had saved his soul, and how God had no part in Peter's sudden death. I—my hair, my time, my witness—was the will of God for Peter.

Hearing and believing is the only means for a person to be saved. But how can they hear without a preacher? 'Preach' simply means 'to tell'. So anyone telling the good news to another is a 'preacher' at that moment. But what if no one tells them? How can they know Jesus if you don't do your Christian duty? What if God's perfect will for another person's salvation is *you*?

Jesus told his disciples, "...The harvest truly is great, but the laborers are few; therefore pray the Lord of the harvest, to send out laborers into His harvest" (Luke 10:2). If we examine the situation Jesus was in when He told his disciples to pray for laborers, we see the shocking truth that at that moment, *there were no laborers*! Actually, there was one—Jesus. And He knew that God needed more, so He told them to pray for some. Then, He pulled a "fast one" on them as He told them they were the answer to their own prayer, and sent them out. Now, praying for laborers is not really the paramount issue anymore because there are hundreds of millions of laborers. Now, the prayer should be, “Pray that the Christians will obey.” Will you be the laborer someone has been praying for?

> **“Nobody made a greater mistake than he who did nothing because he could only do a little.”**
>
> —Edmund Burke

11
Overcoming Frustration

I want to take all the pressure off of your witnessing efforts. This chapter will do it. It substantiates the principle of picking only the ripe tomatoes. I've seen many people (even myself in the past) get so frustrated, intense, and even worried while trying to persuade someone to receive Jesus. But it's so much easier than that.

In the summer of 1999, R.W. Schambach set up a 5,000 seat gospel tent in Harlem, New York, and hired Angelo Mitropoulos to coordinate the evangelism efforts of the crusade. In turn, Angelo hired me to assist him, so we spent our days training people in the day sessions and taking them out to the streets of Harlem to win souls, heal the sick, and give hands-on instruction about doing the works of Jesus. I remember a certain instance where I walked up to a group of about 10 people on the street corner. They were drinking and partying, but I felt to interrupt them. I began to hand them flyers to the crusade and tell them that whatever crisis they had in life, Jesus was their answer. As soon as I began to speak, several of them started laughing, joking, and cussing at me. But that didn't bother me (I know how sinners are. They can't help but sin). After I got a piece of God's Word into each person's hand, I said to the group, "No problem. God bless you guys. I can help you get saved and healed by God if you want, so come find me if you need me." I quickly made my exit and walked down the sidewalk. But about 30 feet away, I heard a guy yelling to me and running after me. One guy had left the group and came to me begging for help. He said, "I don't care about them. I need help. I'm 40 years old, I'm a drug addict, and I'm sick all over—I've got pain running through my whole body. I need God in my life."

> **WITNESS PRINCIPLE 12**
>
> Spend Time Only on Good Ground

How easy. I shared with him the gospel and he immediately confessed Christ as Lord and Savior. Then I laid my hand on his head and commanded the pain and sickness to leave him. As I prayed, He looked up with tears saying, "I feel something. It's going all over me." And within a few seconds it was done. He was healed. He began to bend down and jump up and twist and such. And then he'd repeat it. He had no more pain. Through the tears of joy, his face shown with the glory of God and he was a new creation in Christ. Praise the Lord. Don't ever be moved by the hard-hearted hecklers. Only look for the one who is open.

Our primary command from Jesus is to tell everyone the good news. Just tell them. And this is where some of us can get so discouraged in sharing our faith. When a person doesn't believe or respond to the message, we feel like we've failed. Then we try harder. Instead of just moving on, the believer adds 'worry', 'argue', and 'pray harder' to the simple command of 'go tell'. We waste precious time and effort with people who are not ready for Jesus. And this is the great truth that I found in Scripture: spend time only on good ground.

> **But that on the *good ground* are they, *which in an honest and good heart,* having heard the word, keep it, and bring forth fruit with patience** (Luke 8:15).

Though we are to preach to everyone, only certain individuals are ready at any one time, or as the Bible says, "ordained for eternal life." Those are the ones we are looking to spend time with. We have wasted much time trying to persuade the hard-hearted to receive Christ, when we should have sown the seed, left them alone, and spent our efforts on the ones with an honest and good heart.

You will see this pattern in the Book of Acts. There are several accounts of people who received special attention from God and His servants. And they were always the ones with an honest and good heart. They weren't the mean ones or the scoffers. They weren't the mockers. They weren't the ones who didn't care about God. Instead, they were people who feared God to some degree and were interested in the truth. Look at these scriptures and notice the type of people ready for salvation.

Philip was sent by the angel to intercept the chariot where

> **...a man of Ethiopia, an eunuch of great authority under Candace queen of the Ethiopians, who had charge of all her treasury, and had come to Jerusalem *to worship,* was returning, and sitting in his chariot, he was *reading Isaiah* the prophet...and he *asked Philip* that he would come up and sit with him** (Acts 8:27-31).

Notice that the eunuch was coming to worship, and he actually asked Philip to come help him understand the scriptures. This is much better than having to force the truth on someone, isn't it? Hopefully, our lives exemplify Christ enough for folks to ask us for the gospel.

Cornelius, the first Gentile Peter was sent to, was "A *devout man,* and one that *feared God with all his house,* which *gave much alms* to the people, and *prayed to God always*" (Acts 10:1-2). Notice that he wasn't a rebellious sinner, but rather a God-fearing sinner.

"...Sergius Paulus, a *prudent man*; who called for Barnabas and Saul, and *desired to hear the word of God*" (Acts 13:7). He was asking to hear the truth. If someone is asking you, they are probably ready.

"And a certain woman named Lydia, a seller of purple, of the city of Thyatira, *which worshipped God*, heard us: *whose heart the Lord opened*, that *she attended unto the things* which were spoken of Paul" (Acts 16:14). The Lord had already opened her heart. Watch for that.

After the prison gates opened to free Paul and Silas, the deputy had decided to kill himself to avoid the shame. Notice he wasn't going to lie or run and hide. He seemed honest. *"Sirs, what must I do to be saved?"* Then notice after he was saved, "...he took them the same hour of the night, and washed their stripes...and set meat before them, and rejoiced..." (Acts 16:30-34). What a generous new convert—he was a *good man*.

I point out this pattern in order to save Christians from frustrating experiences with sinners or back-sliders who won't listen. Maybe they will listen later. But, until then, don't push it. God may need time to work on them. So, water the seed from time to time, but don't get frustrated, don't feel like a failure, and don't waste your time.

Though there are exceptions, we should spend most of our time on those who are humble and eager to listen. Even the most hardened sinner goes through a brief process of humility before salvation. Even Paul got knocked off his donkey and humbled in an instant before opening up to the Lord. So be on the lookout for that. Don't *completely* ignore the rebellious and the wicked, but be watching for their ground to moisten before you move in. I believe it will save many frustrating witnessing *and* praying hours.

And it will help us obey Jesus. Jesus actually commanded us not to mess with dogs or pigs, "Do not give what is holy to the dogs; nor cast your pearls before swine, lest they trample them under their feet, and turn and tear you in pieces" (Matthew 7:6).

12

ORDINARY OR SPIRIT–FILLED?

And you shall receive power, after the Holy Spirit has come upon you, and you shall be witnesses unto Me... (Acts 1:8).

The Holy Spirit is the catalyst for the power. He is the spiritual Doer of the deed. And we must be close to Him. We must be full of Him. We must be filled with the holy fire of the Spirit. And that requires some discipline in lifestyle and in prayer. Either we're strong in spirit, or we're weaklings. And you can't be a weakling and still help people. You can't break the devil's power if you're not ready. And your faith will faint if you don't stay stirred up.

Ordinary Christians don't do well at witnessing. They are too rough and argumentative, too hard, and too carnal with their attitude and message. And they are too care*less*. I want to help you *not be* ordinary! But *extra-ordinary* requires a life that is fueled by the Holy Spirit. The scriptures speak of the outward man and the inward man, "...though our outward man perishes, yet the inward man is renewed day by day..." (2 Corinthians 4:16). The inward man is our spirit, who lives connected to the Holy Spirit. When our spirit is full of the Holy Spirit, it can reach out and touch people. But if it is not, then our carnal nature (our outward man) becomes a hindrance to us and we remain lazy, stingy, and mean. Lazy and stingy people can't bless others, and they're never blessed by God. On the other hand, on-fire spiritual people are both blessed by God and also a blessing to others. It is our outward man that thinks he's so clever and cute. It's our outward man that wears the armor of pride. It's our outward man that trembles in fear, because it is weak. It's our outward man that parades its personality more than the love of God.

WITNESS PRINCIPLE 13

The Power You Have Is for Witnessing

But if we stay close to the scriptures and fervent in Spirit-filled prayer, our inward man can break forth in coming to the triumphant rescue of people. A Spirit-filled person can put his arms around people and let the love of God minister. A Spirit-filled person is in tune with the Spirit.

If we remain dull and ordinary, the world loses its chance for salvation. That's what happened in developed countries like England, Germany, and even Australia. The gospel once rang freely there through some powerful moves of God. But human efficiency and intellectual enlightenment gave believers something else to do, and to a large degree, those countries lost their Christian flavor for many decades. America has the potential for that as well, but we've held on to enough hot wood to keep some fires burning.

But if we accept this glorious call to power, our witness will be clear. We won't think of it as *doing* witnessing activities, but rather as *being* what the Spirit made us. So, don't grow cold. Don't get lukewarm. If you feel yourself growing indifferent, get back to your Bible reading. Get back to daily prayer. Pray in tongues more. Fast one day a week. Or fast the beginning of each month. And certainly stay connected to and active in church—one that believes in the power of God and the great commission. And stir yourself back up to serve the living God. Backsliders and lukewarm Christians don't feel like doing much spiritually. But if you'll do it by faith, God will meet you, those wonderful holy feelings will come back, and sharing your faith will have a spark of the supernatural rather than the dullness of a forced, dreaded, burdensome task.

We need a burning fire for people. We need a heart cry for the world, for the lost, for the hurting. We need to get back to loving *and* liking people. We need to be genuinely concerned that hell is a real place where unbelievers go. This is called compassion. And only the Holy Spirit can fill us with the compassion of Jesus. "...the love of God is shed abroad in our hearts by the Holy Ghost which is given unto us" (Romans 5:5). True compassion (not sympathy) is a spiritual force that will not allow us to pass the sinner by without sharing this wonderful gospel of love and power. Our heart should consider their eternal soul. We should care where people are spiritually. We should want them to have a better day, to have a better life, to have eternal hope, confidence and joy, to understand God rightly, and to escape hell.

Compassion carries the atmosphere for miracles. It can do that because it's not a *natural* thing. Instead, it is very *super*-natural; it comes only from heaven. Love is the very nature of God ("...*for God is love*"). "The Lord is gracious and full of compassion..." (Psalm 145:8-9). Jesus was motivated by this compassion. If you study it, many times he was *moved with compassion* before He worked a miracle. He healed the leper and the blind men and delivered the demoniac because of compassion. He fed the multitude because of compassion.

He raised the dead woman's son because of compassion. He stilled the storms because of compassion. And if you want to work miracles and help on this earth in any capacity, it must be from the motivation of compassion—not fame, not glory, but with the same spiritual motivator that Jesus had—compassion.

I once knew a precious lady named Vicky who would frequent the most dangerous places in Houston, sharing Christ with the homeless, the drug addicts, and the thugs. With a loving smile and great, holy tenderness, she would approach any of them and say with her sweet Spanish accent, "Do you have Jesus in your heart?" Many would melt at the love of God and be saved.

God's nature is in us. But we can't let it lie dormant. We've got to stir it up! "But ye, beloved, building up yourselves on your most holy faith, praying in the Holy Ghost, Keep yourselves in the love of God..." (Jude 20, 21). The sure way to keep ourselves full of compassion is to be praying in the Spirit—not once or twice a week, but daily, continually. If we Spirit-filled Christians do not pray in the Holy Spirit (in tongues) consistently, we can be assured that our compassion for people is dwindling and our efforts are becoming works in the flesh. It takes discipline. It requires real effort to set aside time to force your flesh to sit down a while and let your spirit pray in the Holy Spirit every day, but the benefit is God's abiding presence and a sweet compassion for people.

"But I don't feel anything. I feel dry. I don't feel like the Spirit's leading me. I don't feel the anointing. I don't feel any love. What if nothing happens?"

It will.

You're partially right, before you talk to someone, before you step out, before you approach, there is no power evident. There is no tangible feeling of power present until the Word of God is preached. Until the Spirit knows you are stepping out to share something with someone, He will lie dormant inside you. He may be speaking to you about your own life or reminding you of your walk with God, but He will not be giving you any special anointing or grace to witness to another. So, you may feel very dry and natural. But if you tell the gospel, power comes!

WITNESS PRINCIPLE 14

No Power Until You Speak

> **The preaching of the cross is foolishness to those who are perishing, but to us who are saved *it is the power of God*** (1 Corinthians 1:18).

Remember, the Holy Spirit is *your* Helper. You are not *His*. He may nudge you and remind you of your witness or of someone particular, but He will patiently wait to give His anointing until you decide to step out. Once you get into a conversation, all of a sudden He is there, and the ministry to the person begins. You might not even remember a scripture until you get in and need it. You might feel as blank and dry as ever until a lost person dips into that *well of life* inside you and God comes flowing out. Remember that it is the Lord's work and we are just the vessels. He who is in you is the One who carries out the spiritual completion. Remembering that will relieve us of pressure and also give us confidence that the power and the right words will be there on time.

It is the same with preaching in a pulpit or to a crowd. Most of the time, the preacher feels nothing—zero, dry as a bone, sometimes nervous—until he or she steps onto the platform. The anointing is not some goosey feeling that tells us if something will happen. Rather, it is the ability and power that flows once someone is open to receive ministry. One way that you can tell if someone is closed to the Lord is that the anointing seems to be stuck, or stifled, or dried up. When the flow of ministry seems gone, either cease in that moment, or pray silently that God will open the person's soul to receive.

(Wait…as I type this, one of our fired up church members just phone texted me and said he just led the rental car attendant at the Dallas airport to the Lord…she had thought she was being "good enough" for salvation, but then believed the message he shared of Jesus being the only way, and received Him. Praise the Lord. And now another text from him: the bus driver to the rental car just got saved! And now another: the rental car checkout attendant just accepted Christ! Three in a row for this new soul-winner—now that's living life!)

> **"Do all the good you can, by all the means you can, in all the ways you can, to all the people you can, in all the places you can, to all the people you can, as long as ever you can."**
>
> —John Wesley

> **"Before you are filled with the Spirit, don't go. After you are filled with the Spirit, don't stay."**
>
> —Unknown

13
Your Sphere of Influence

Every believer has a sphere of influence, a proximity to the world that is unique and divinely planned. This is *your* world. You are in it, and others are in it—family and friends, co-workers and neighbors, and strangers and acquaintances. And they are yours—your people, your call, your responsibility. And whether they are sinners, back-sliders, or nominal, careless Christians, they need you. Each sphere group requires a somewhat different approach, so be familiar with them.

Family and Friends

Family and friends are usually the most challenging group of sinners we attempt to turn to Christ. Ironically, they are the ones that we tend to pounce on first. The natural reaction to this great salvation is to immediately run to our favorite people and share the news. And I say *go for it.* It would be wrong to instruct new Christians to delay their witness to family and friends for some arbitrary moment out in the future—you know, "after you've been educated and such." New Christians are going to blab the news. And they should. It's too good to hold it in. And there is no need for me to warn you of what's going to happen, for if you are already saved, then you've already noticed: your people didn't all share in your enthusiasm, did they?

So, your family didn't throw you a parade and run to the store to buy themselves a Bible and some church clothes, and give their life to the Lord? No problem. After the new believer realizes (usually the hard way) that pearls and swine don't mix, he must change his strategy. Family and friends may take time. And our regurgitation of what we just learned at church is not what they will usually respond to first. They know you just learned it, so give it some time to take root in you. You may be giving the most anointed replay of a certain Bible truth on Sunday afternoon, but all they hear is, "I'm now something that you're not, everything you thought you knew about God is wrong, and here, let me prove to you how right I am, blah blah blah." To you, the light has shined and the kingdom of God has become real. But

WITNESS PRINCIPLE 15

Your World is Your Responsibility

to them, you've just gone crazy. You now see all the new things in Christ and the new possibilities for your holy transformation. But your family and closest friends have a different perspective. They see the same old you. Though your exuberance may be something new, your history hasn't changed. It will somctimes require a few pages of the calendar to turn before they recognize the real soul change inside you. And that is the key with family and friends. It may take time and consistency.

During that time, they will be watching your every move, secretly listening to your conversations, and evaluating everything in your life. Are you really different now, or just loony? Are you seriously committed to God, or will you turn out a hypocrite? Is the church you get up for every Sunday morning an honest place, or is it full of charlatans?

They won't be looking at you as their teacher. They will be looking at your lifestyle. And this is where your witness must turn into the love of God. This is where your gospel presentation becomes your life rather than your words. And this is where the rubber meets the road. If you are a hearer and not a doer, your old man will remain alive and your people will know it. This is clearly noted in Ralph Waldo Emerson's famous quote, "What you do speaks so loudly, I can't hear what you are saying." Or how about this one by Pink Floyd, The Wall, "Your lips move, but I can't hear what you are saying."

With family and friends, you will need to begin with one thing: love them. Be kind to them. Treat them much better than before you were saved. Speak less. Do more. And change your attitude toward them. Be good to them. It's the *goodness of God that leads men to repentance.* Allow God to do his divine thing in them and open their heart. And never let them see you blow it. Or better yet, just never blow it. If you do, repent immediately. And apologize to them, again, immediately. Apologizing for your rudeness (or any sins against them) will go a long way in winning them to Christ because it reveals a tender spirit that has been touched by God. If you've already beat up most of your family and friends with the Bible, start now on your new pattern of lifestyle witnessing. God can recover them.

Only speak when they will listen. Only answer when they ask. And wait for the door to open. If they barely crack the door, don't barge in and dump all of your information on them at once. Remember, they don't see you as their teacher. Don't blab everything that you're learning, nor testify of all your intimate experiences with God. Rather, wait. When the time is right, toss some breadcrumbs and see if they'll grab them. Throw some bait and see if they're hungry. And be patient. Be wise. If you will allow the Lord Jesus Christ to fill you with love and transform you into His image, they will see. And then they will have a chance to follow. Hopefully, you are going to church consistently and they can follow you there.

Don't get me wrong about this. A passive witnessing lifestyle is necessary for daily living. But at some point, you will absolutely need to say something on purpose. Jesus went around saying things about God, seeing who He could catch. So should we, for no one can be saved until they hear the gospel. Just be wise in choosing your preaching moments. And be ready to cease any conversation that isn't headed the direction you want it.

Also, don't be hyper-spiritual, don't be weird, and no showing off. Don't do anything spiritual, like praying or worshipping, with the secret motive of them seeing you. And don't coerce *them* to do anything spiritual, for spiritual things are impossible to the one who is asleep unto God. So, no need to force everyone to let you pray out loud at dinner. And no need to purposely leave your Bible lying around the house, open to the page you think they need to read. Recognize that only God can open their hearts, and until He does so, your manipulation will just appear odd and childish.

I want you to know this, though. Your people want you to make it! Secretly, deep down, far below all their hardness and apathy, they are rooting for you. They want you to be a successful Christian. That little "God-shaped hole" in every man's heart silently yearns for someone on this earth to do it right—to be connected to the holy God, to live above the fallen world, and to demonstrate Godly love and goodness without hypocrisy. If you do it right, you will be their champion, and they can follow you to Christ. If you are weird or harsh, they won't.

The Bible even addresses an unbelieving *spouse*, and explains that that a meek and humble spirit can entice them to the Lord, without any words, but by chaste conduct (1 Peter 3:1-3). Every married person wants their spouse to join them on their spiritual journey. But you can't force it. Be patient, love them, serve the Lord without them, and hopefully they will eventually come along.

Co-Workers and Neighbors

Co-workers and neighbors are a bit different than your closest family and friends because they don't get to see the personal side of your life quite as often. But they do see you consistently. So, your first witness style is love. Walk in love. And again, never blow it. If you do, again, please apologize immediately for your lack of consideration for them or your dishonor of God. This can be applied even to strangers who see you frequently. Stay alert to the Image you reflect.

My wife, Joni, tells of a certain gas station cashier on whom she had spent some focused witnessing effort, on several encounters. Each time, she had been very cheerful and inspiring, to the point that he had asked why she was so happy. That gave her the opportunity to give a reason for "the hope that is within her"—that her joy was because of her good God—how He loved her and was so kind to her, and that's why she's always cheerful. However, one day she went into the store with a somewhat neutral, disengaged look on her face (for no real reason, probably just lost in daily activities). The cashier asked, "Why aren't you cheerful today? Is your God not good anymore?" What a wake-up. Clearly, how we act toward and appear to others matters in presenting an attractive, consistent image of God. And once you decide to light your world, you'll recognize how significant your daily walk can be to people.

Look for opportunities to share Christ with them or challenge their careless attitude about God. Be led by the Spirit and wait for right moments when you can speak to the right ones. But don't expect to wait long. We don't have to be as constrained with this group because it's easier for them (and us) to walk away if they're not interested in Christ. Be open and honest, and be sensitive to their attention and demeanor. Lead them to pray for salvation the moment you find out they believe the message of Jesus Christ.

And one more tip: usually, it's best to pick them off one by one rather than address a group that is together. Together, sinners are less likely to converse openly with you. And they are more inclined to either show off to the group, protect their image with pride or silence, or even feel strength in numbers and use one another to resist you. I have seen those who are quite uneasy when they are approached with friends present, thinking that their reputation might be in jeopardy if they show any interest. But, as soon as they are alone, they freely open up. If you do have the opportunity to speak to a group (or couple) at once, be aware of who is open and listening, and find them later for a more personal discussion.

After I re-dedicated my life to the Lord, I was soon sent to Atlanta, Georgia on a year-long consulting project for a certain client. Our project team consisted of about 20 people, most of which were not believers and none of which were serving the Lord in a real way. So, it was perfectly clear to me: this was my field of souls. I didn't pounce on them with preaching. Rather, I waited. I practiced my love walk. I allowed the Spirit of God to help me be the model Christian. I was nice and gentle. I was patient and kind. I never retaliated for wrongs nor showed any anger. One time at lunch I told a funny story of my roommate (also my co-worker and also present) to a group of our team. But it wasn't funny to him, and I noticed he didn't appreciate me telling it. Once back at the office, I was sitting at my desk feeling really guilty and sad for hurting my roommate's feelings. I asked God to forgive me. But then God pulled me further. As I was praying about it, my roommate walked over to our common area printer, right next to my desk. And I knew what I had to do. I walked over to him and said, "I'm sorry for what I said in the car. I think it might have hurt you, and I shouldn't have done that. Please forgive me." He smiled and said that it did hurt him, but that he would forgive me. Glory! God's Spirit rushed over me! And I knew I had preserved the gospel seed in my roommate's soul.

During that time, I always asked the Lord to help me pick them off one at a time. And I waited. I shared Christ with almost all of them eventually. But most of my work was the preparation—the lifestyle, the love, the commitment to their eternal destiny. When the project ended and I was packing up to head home, one of the guys shook my hand and said, "Chas, you're the first real Christian I have ever known, aside from my grandfather. Thank you for being a genuine example of what you believe." Praise the Lord. I had fulfilled my call from heaven.

I loved the workplace environment. I thought it a great honor to be called by God to a specific group of employees. Some of the most fun I ever had was the challenge of loving lost people day after day and working with the Spirit to win them to Christ. For me, it was a bitter sweet day when the Lord directed me to leave my career for full time ministry. I felt great knowing I was obeying God, but I was fully cognizant of what I was having to give up. I would never again experience the secular workplace witnessing ride again. (Whatever situation you are in, enjoy the ride.)

And think of this. If God's top priority is in spreading His good news, it would be more important than the promotion or the better job you want, right? Since it is so, then if you'll take on this call as a witness to those God has placed in proximity to you, you can change jobs quicker. If you'll hurry up and witness right to everyone at work, He will promote you sooner. If you're not faithful with your current people, God isn't much interested in sending you to a new group of people. Or we could view it even more severely: if your current people are seeing a dimly lit, lukewarm Christian at work, why would God want to let a new group of people see that? He wouldn't. He'd just keep you there so no one else gets tainted with so-so Christianity. Doesn't this logical, spiritual deduction make sense? And doesn't it reveal how the great commission really is higher priority than our other "doings"?

Strangers and Acquaintances

Strangers and acquaintances will be the ones that get to hear the gospel from you the quickest. You may not see them ever again. They will have no chance to analyze your love walk or examine your character. One chance, then it's over. So tell them the gospel on your first meeting. Don't wait. Don't wonder about it. Just do it. Ask them if they're saved. Tell them what to believe. See if they believe it. And lead them to pray if they do. Maybe you bumped into them this one time as God's lone chance to give them the good news. Don't pass it up. Tell them all. Maybe you get into a good conversation and can teach them some details of the kingdom or something, but maybe not. At least give them the first message—the gospel of salvation, healing, and deliverance.

Oh, did I mention that this group is also the scariest? At least at first, strangers seem to be so intimidating for us to talk to about the Lord. It really should be the opposite, since if we mess up, we'll never see them again anyway. But for some reason, Christians shake in their boots at the thought of approaching a stranger with a gospel tract or a conversation about Jesus. Don't let it happen to you. You are empowered by the Spirit of God to open your mouth and let Him minister to sinners. Your words don't have to be perfect. You could even stutter and forget things. You could do it in broken English or terrible Spanish. But if you do it with compassion and sincerity, the Spirit will convince and save them.

I remember the first person I ever personally led to the Lord. In my third or fourth month in the kingdom of God, I was in downtown Houston walking back to the office after lunch. A man about 21 years old approached me, asking for money. And as I reached in my pocket, I began to talk with him about the Lord. He explained to me that it would be impossible for him to be forgiven because he had killed people. Not as a murderer, but as a soldier in the Russian army. And he felt terribly guilty for it. He had been staying at a shelter, where he had heard a few things about Jesus. But he felt no hope to be saved. I gave him some. I told him that first of all, fulfilling a governmental duty of keeping order and peace does not violate the command of God. And second, Jesus died for exactly the thing that he needed—the freedom from guilt and penalty. He prayed to receive Christ with tears of joy. And then went on his way.

One day I had a little free time during an all day faith conference, so I visited the nearby mall. I walked in one of the main entrances near the food court and just opened up to the Lord thinking, *well, maybe I could find someone to share Christ with.* I don't always do this because my *flesh* isn't usually interested in sharing Christ. My flesh would be more interested in the food and the buying of material things. But my *spirit* was ready (it's always ready, just like yours). I looked around and found a young man sitting at a table eating lunch by himself. I walked over and politely asked him if I might sit down with him and share something with him. He threw his lunch at me, called the police, and started jumping up and down like a monkey, laughing at me. No, just kidding. Of course not. Sinners practically never do anything belligerent to you. He actually said, "Sure, have a seat." So I sat down and began to ask him questions about his belief in Jesus Christ. Come to find out, he had recently attended a large, Spirit-filled church a couple times, seeking the truth. But he had not responded to the message. He certainly believed in Jesus, but he had not put it all together yet and found the courage to make a decision. So, I helped him do the right thing. He prayed to receive Christ there at the table. And I could see that he was relieved and happy about his decision. I almost baptized him in the mall fountain, but we both decided maybe that wasn't best.

Not to frighten you further, but just in case you are feeling a burning in your heart to do this, here are some opening lines you can use out there:

1. Are you saved?
2. I'd like to share something with you. Got a minute?
3. I want to tell you some good news. May I?
4. God bless you today. Do you believe in God? What do you know about Jesus?
5. Do you know anything about God, or the Bible?
6. May I tell you some exciting news—the best news you'll ever hear?

The truth is, you can open up a conversation with almost anything, and people will many times respond. The amazing thing, once you commit to sharing your faith, is how easy it is and how open many people are to letting you speak about Jesus.

14
How Do I Know If the Lord Is Leading Me?

Without going into the basics of how Christians can be led by the Spirit of God in daily life, I want to describe two helpful secrets when it comes to noticing when the Lord is moving you to minister to someone. Though occasionally we might hear a *sentence* from God, what we usually get is only a *sense*. And sometimes we don't even get that. I have learned that one way the Holy Spirit leads us to certain witnessing encounters is by chance meetings or strange events, which turn out to be divine set-ups. These are those situations where we think, *Hmm, now that's odd...*

Now, throughout the day, I don't believe that every single step the Christian takes is some divine appointment of God that requires us to do something spiritual. And I don't believe the popular myth that "everything happens for a reason." But on the other hand, some things are absolutely

planned by God, and if our spiritual eye blinks, we'll miss them. Brother Kenneth Hagin always said, "Many folks are looking for the spectacular, but missing the supernatural every day."

For instance, one day at the airport waiting for my plane, I found myself sitting next to a lady in the waiting area. I was looking for a chance, or a leading, to share Christ with her, but I didn't have any particular open door. Eventually, the plane arrived, and we boarded and found our seats on the plane. And out of over 140 seats, guess who I'm sitting next to? The same lady. Now that could be a coincidence, but since I'm walking with God and expecting to help everyone I can every day, I felt it was a Holy Spirit encounter. This gave me great faith that whatever I said would be right, and powerful, and ordained by God. The lady didn't give her life to Christ on the plane, but the ministry to her was pure and planted firmly.

Remember, not every person we are led to share with will receive Christ. Jesus was led by the Spirit every day, and many rejected Him to His face. Paul was led to many cities, arrested and stoned in some of them, but we can't say he missed God or ministered poorly. God will lead us to many people, and our success is not determined by their response. Our success is determined by "Did we do God's will of giving *all* people the chance to believe the gospel?"

One day a friend of mine came to my gospel print shop just to say hello. He brought two of his teenage nephews with him, so I shut the printing press off and began to talk with them. Before long I realized this was an odd thing for strangers to be in my 12 ft. by 10 ft. print shop, so I knew something was about to happen. In the middle of a print job, with my gloved hands covered with ink, I decided to show the boys what I was printing. It was a gospel tract that says *"This is Your Life, What is Next."* As they read the newly printed literature, I quickly shared with them how to be saved. I then asked them, "Would you like to be saved now?" One of the boys looked up at me and said, "I think I just was." Hallelujah! The one boy had believed in his heart so strongly that he felt the change had begun within him even before he prayed. I went ahead and had both of the boys call upon the name of the Lord out loud so I could hear them, and they were both born again.

It's not enough for people to *only* believe. To complete the miracle of salvation, it requires a belief first, and then 'saying it' second (Romans 10:9-10). One of our church members, who was recently saved and filled with the Spirit, had taken a step to share Christ with two of her co-workers. She gave them a gospel tract and watched them read it. They both believed it and thanked her. She went home to tell her husband the good news, but her husband wanted her to go back and make them pray out loud. The next day, she boldly approached the two co-workers and told them they needed to read the prayer out loud to God. As they did, they both began crying and rejoicing at the same time. And they were saved. Always get people to confess Christ out loud (see Chapter 25).

Consider the devil possessed fortuneteller that followed Paul for many days, crying "These men are the servants of the most high God which shew unto us the way of salvation" (Acts 16:17). Now that's a little strange for a devil-possessed lady to be helping a preacher, but Paul was wise enough to notice it. After allowing it to continue for many days, Paul was grieved and moved to solve the problem. He cast the devil out of her, and she was freed.

I believe that Jesus recognized it somewhat strange for the Samaritan woman to be coming to the well at the noon hour in John Chapter 4 (most ladies filled their water pots in the morning). Just as I had faith on the airplane because I recognized God was involved, I believe Jesus recognized the high probability that He would help the woman who had come for water at such an odd hour of the day.

Another time I was shopping in a Lowe's store when another customer approached me. He was shopping on the same aisle with me and had found a great sale price on an item. He was overly excited about it and began to share his joy with me, how this item cost such-n-such more at another store, but here it was about half that, and so on. In a few minutes, I had heard of his job, his recent marriage, his name, and his life travels. This was fairly strange, since I didn't ask him for the information, so I perked up my spiritual antenna and re-directed the conversation. I soon found out that he had just started going to a Catholic church because his new wife "liked to pray every night." He believed in Christ but was not saved, so I just helped him receive Christ right there in the store. He was saved. Praise the Lord.

Smith Wigglesworth tells a story of one of these strange encounters.

> When I was going out to Australia recently, our boat stopped at Aden and at Bombay. In the first place the people came round the ship selling their wares, beautiful carpets and all sorts of oriental things. There was one man selling some ostrich feathers. As I was looking over the side of the ship watching the trading, a gentleman said to me, "Would you go shares with me in buying that bunch of feathers?" What did I want with feathers? I had no use for such things and no room for them either. But the gentleman put the question to me again, "Will you go shares with me in buying that bunch?" The Spirit of God said to me, "Do it."
>
> The feathers were sold to us for three pounds, and the gentleman said, "I have no money on me, but if you will pay the man for them, I will send the cash down to you by

> the purser." I paid for the feathers and gave the gentleman his share. He was traveling first, and I was traveling second class. I said to him, "No, please don't give that money to the purser, I want you to bring it to me personally to my cabin." I said to the Lord, "What about these feathers?" He showed me that He had a purpose in my purchasing them.
>
> At about 10 o'clock the gentleman came to my cabin and said, "I've brought the money." I said to him, "It is not your money that I want, it is your soul that I am seeking for God." Right there he opened up the whole plan of his life and began to seek God; and that morning he wept his way through to God's salvation (Wigglesworth, p. 99).

Keep on the lookout for chance encounters where someone chooses you out of a crowd to ask directions, or where some stranger begins to tell you their life story out of the blue, or where you find yourself with a person who has an honest heart and wants to talk. Or even if you're interrupted by a flat tire or something, be on the lookout to witness. I've learned that if I'm faithful to share Christ with people during any odd circumstance, the odd circumstance will alleviate itself much quicker. Many times, I know that it is God who has brought the right person to us in our interruption. (But make no mistake here, I am not saying that God ever causes us evil or pain to help us reach a sinner. That would go against His good nature and His covenant promises of blessing and protection. And God will never break one covenant promise to fulfill another. Common tribulation, such as home repairs or long lines at the grocery store, is what I'm talking about, rather than uncommon tragedies like hospital emergencies or funerals.) Don't make the mistake of waiting for a booming voice from heaven before you share the gospel. Instead, keep your spiritual antenna up and watch for strange events. Let me say it again. *There will be no booming voice telling you to witness.*

> **But ye have an anointing (an unction) from the Holy One, and you know all things…But the anointing which you have received from Him abides in you…** (1 John 2:20-27).

The anointing that we speak much of is actually found only a couple times in Scripture, and it refers to the presence of the Holy Ghost within the believer. That impulse, or "tug", or prompting from God is how we are to be led by the Spirit. It is the 'inward witness' or the 'inward director'. Sometimes, this impulse is a solid 'knowing' of what to do. Other times it is an even larger, more overwhelming compulsion from the Spirit. And sometimes it may feel only like a little flutter that comes up from your spirit, where you feel as if you just have a sudden urge to do something. I call it a *holy urge*.

Here is an example. One day I was driving home on the Houston freeway, and I had this sudden desire to go buy an ice cream cone from Marble Slab Creamery (where they mix the ice cream with any topping you wish). Now, if you are one who eats special ice cream all the time, then maybe it wouldn't happen to you like this. But for me, this was very abnormal since at that time I rarely went there to get ice cream; I have always thought of it as more of a special occasion place to go. But I made the exit and went to get my treat. I had planned to buy the ice cream and eat it on the way home, but it was the middle of summer and scorching hot. So, as I walked outside, the ice cream began to run all down my hand. I decided to stand outside and finish it. But as I was standing there, I heard someone call my name, "Hey Chas!" I turned to see an old friend from high school that I hadn't seen in 10 years. You

WITNESS PRINCIPLE 17

Watch for Holy Urges

know, in a large city like Houston, you can go years without ever seeing someone you know out in public. We greeted each other and he asked what I was doing now. Rather than say that I'm a preacher, I just began with, "Well, I got saved by God a few years ago, and He changed my life and healed me from allergies. And now I'm trying to help others get saved and healed by God."

My friend's response was, "Hey, you know, the same thing happened to Roger" (one of our mutual friends who had planted seed in this guy already). And I was able to share the gospel with him. He didn't choose to receive Christ at the time, but I know that the Lord had specifically sent me, not to fatten up on ice cream, but to help nurture the gospel seed in this sinner. The same thing happened to me about a year later while I was with my friend, Mark. We were driving in the car deciding where to eat, and we settled on James Coney Island. But for us, that was an odd choice, since we didn't even know where a single James Coney Island was located. So we just picked a major street in Houston, Texas, and started driving, looking for hot dogs. We ended up driving and driving for miles, wondering if we would ever find a James Coney Island, and wondering why we didn't want to just change our minds and go elsewhere. As we drove, we were just talking about the Lord, and I shared my ice cream story with Mark, just for fun. Soon after, we found a James Coney restaurant. As we walked in, a person at the first nearby table hollered my name, "Chas!" It was another of my friends from high school! In an instant, Mark and I both knew why we had such an unction to find a James Coney Island, so we had great confidence to speak to my high school friend. He asked what I was doing these days, and I said, "Well, I don't know if you heard, but I gave my life to Jesus Christ and now I'm preaching the gospel and helping others get saved. And it seems the Lord sent us here to talk to you." We talked for only a minute or two, planted some solid gospel seed in my friend. And then we headed for our hot dogs. Though my friend did not accept Christ at that moment, we knew we had followed the will of God by way of the subtle, inward nudge of the Holy Spirit and accomplished our goal.

One time I was wade fishing out in the surf in Galveston, Texas. I had caught a half stringer of speckled trout and was headed for a limit of ten (which, if you're from this area, you know is one of the premier goals of sport fishing). But all of a sudden, I had this overwhelming urge to leave. I knew it was God. I stopped fishing and walked out of the water. As soon as I reached dry land, a guy in a pickup truck drove by and stopped with his window down. I knew that I had to talk with him about the Lord, so I walked over to him. The first thing he said was that he had cancer and didn't have long to live. I preached Christ to him, prayed with him, cursed the cancer, and instructed him to read a certain portion of the Bible to help him believe. He drove off, and I headed back to the beach house to clean my fish, knowing exactly what that internal, electric urge I had was all about. Notice that being led by God doesn't mean you get to know everything at once. Rather, He leads us step by step, and wants us to obey each without knowing the next. I mean, God wanted me to halt my successful fishing moment for no apparent reason. I had to obey before knowing why. That is called faith—not blind faith, there's no such thing, but hearing from God and believing without seeing beforehand.

We need to grow and practice in knowing which plans are of God and which ones we incorrectly force upon ourselves. Sometimes we make a phone call because we feel guilty for not keeping contact with someone. Or we make a decision out of pressure. Our heart doesn't really feel right about it, and we dread and procrastinate for weeks before finally forcing ourselves to do it. Really, that lack of freedom and desire to do something is the Spirit of God directing us *away* from it. Don't let your smart head override your knowing heart, and don't let the fear of man be larger than your desire to obey God. The real you down on the inside is who should make the decision. (There is much more to know about being led by the Spirit, but if you'll make a commitment to learn His voice and allow Him to be your Helper, you'll get there.)

15
What If They Reject Me?

Okay Christians, let's talk about our feelings. And then let's say good-bye to them. Feelings have little or no place in sharing our faith. There's no crying in...soul-winning. Remember, this is a *strong man's gospel.* Come on, be strong, and take it like a Christian.

> **Blessed are ye, when men shall revile you, and persecute you, and shall say all manner of evil against you falsely, for my sake. *Rejoice, and be exceeding glad:* for great is your reward in heaven: for so persecuted they the prophets which were before you** (Matthew 5:11-12).

Did you see that? Jesus wants us to rejoice and be glad about it.

But that sounds a little strange, doesn't it? If you've ever been rejected or made fun of for the gospel's sake, you'll know that to *rejoice* is a very unnatural emotional reaction. Our flesh wants to shrink and hide. But this gospel is not natural. Rather, it is very *super*natural. Everything we do must be done by faith. Faith put to action will always contradict the

> **Witness Principle 18**
>
> Bye Bye Feelings

direction our flesh would prefer to take.

And notice: *it is a direct command from Jesus that we rejoice*. We must *force* ourselves to rejoice. Only then can we receive the real blessing that rises within our heart for obeying God. If we keep a spiritual heading about it, we'll remember that there is "*...great reward in heaven*" awaiting us. Knowing that will sustain us through all gospel difficulties with family and friends. You may feel like a failure when they don't believe you, when they scoff at you, or when you're unable to convince them to receive Christ. But you're in good company. Sinners, as well as traditional religious people, rejected Jesus, too.

Stephen, the martyr, and every other believer murdered for the gospel's sake, seemed to be failures to the natural world. But they weren't. In fact, those that appear to be least will actually be the greatest. There is even a special martyrs' crown given in heaven. But most of us will never die for our faith, so we don't even need to consider that. Then again, if we contemplate the ultimate persecution of death, it may seem to the wimpy Christian that death would be easier to take than to suffer rejection in front of his friends. (You can get mad at me for using the word 'wimpy' if you want to. That's why I used it—I'm trying to stir you up. If Jesus were here, He might say something like, "O ye of little faith..." Would you like that any better?)

Come on! Let's act supernatural about it. Make a decision to take it on the cheek for Jesus' sake. Look at the faith and boldness of the early Church, and let's contend for that.

> **...and when they had called the apostles, and beaten them, they commanded that they should not speak in the name of Jesus, and let them go. And they departed from the presence of the council, *rejoicing that they were***

> ***counted worthy to suffer shame for His name*** (Acts 5:40-41).
>
> **But the Jews stirred up the devout and honourable women, and the chief men of the city, and raised persecution against Paul and Barnabas, and expelled them out of their coasts. But they *shook off the dust of their feet against them,* and came unto Iconium. And *the disciples were filled with joy, and with the Holy Ghost*** (Acts 13:50-52).

Look at that. They got kicked out of the city and were filled with…sadness? No, they were filled with *joy*. It takes faith to think like that. Apparently they knew Jesus, and apparently they had revelation of this strong man's gospel. You can, too.

I read a story long ago about a Christian woman in Germany who approached a homeless man who had been sleeping on a park bench. She handed him a gospel tract. But when he saw what it was, he berated her and yelled, "I don't want this!", and threw it on the ground. The rejection crushed her, and she walked off crying. What she didn't know was that as she turned away, the wind blew the little gospel paper back under the man's feet. He then kicked the tract the other direction, but the wind blew it right back under his feet. So, he picked it up, read it, and accepted Jesus Christ while sitting on that bench. The man was delivered from alcohol, soon became a preacher, and travelled all over Germany preaching the gospel. In every church, he would end the meeting by telling the story of how he was saved and of the lady who was sincere enough to share the gospel with him. He wanted to find her and thank her. He did this for seven years, until one day at the end of a church service, a tearful woman approached him and admitted she was the one. She said that she was so embarrassed and disappointed from how he had rejected her that she had never again witnessed to anyone for all those seven years. Seven years!

Hopefully, she was able to pick up where she left off. And hopefully, we know enough to avoid the same trap of disappointment. Never underestimate the power of the Word of God when given to another. And never be sad when you're rejected.

> **And whosoever shall not receive you, nor hear you, when ye depart thence, *shake off the dust under your feet for a testimony against them*...** (Mark 6:11).

What an odd thing for Jesus to say. I wonder why he didn't say, "If they don't accept you, pray for them as you leave, and ask God to have mercy on them anyway"?

Isn't that what we usually do? We feel some religious duty or emotional distress to pray for them? Sometimes, our compassion may cause us to pray for them. But other times that is the wrong reaction. Jesus said to shake the dust off our feet, and get out of there. Now, in this country, the "shaking the dust" term may be a little blind to us. But it refers to us cutting off our tie to the heathen who won't listen—to come out from among them and be separate and to decontaminate our minds from their rejection. And Jesus said this must be done for a *testimony against them*, to testify before heaven and earth that this person (or people) has made their decision to reject God.

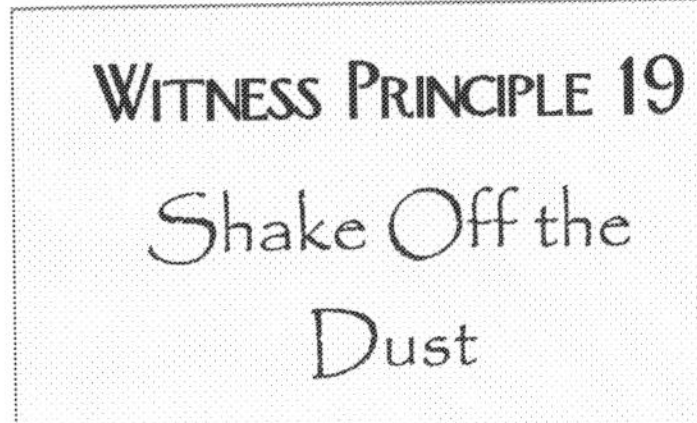

At the least, we must not "cast our pearls before swine" (Matthew 7:6). But that is what happens so often, especially with our family members. We care about them so much that we ignore what Jesus said. And we grovel to God about them for years, wasting much of our prayer time and our ministry on someone who is not ready. Our determination for a certain person many times turns into anxiety and disappointment, causing us to remain perpetually worried that salvation may never come for them. And therefore God cannot get involved because we're in the way. (We'll discuss how to pray effectively for family in a later chapter.)

I'm not saying that we should rudely turn our face from all those who won't receive Jesus. I'm not saying that we have to be mean to people or quit loving them. But there is a time to visibly separate one's self from the rejecters until they come around. There are different levels of rebellion, and you'll have to discern which warrants a more firm disconnect. The point is that we must get a better picture of the precise contrast of righteousness vs. unrighteousness. We are carriers of the salvation of God, the Christ, the Holy One who has extended His merciful arm to mankind. When His arm is rejected, He pulls it back—at least for a season. They may have another chance later. But if God pulls back and wants a testimony *against* them, I believe we are in a desert place if we do not also pull back. There is a time to stop talking. There is a time to stop praying for them. If you want a scripture for this, "God resists the proud, But gives grace to the humble" (James 4:6). If God resists some people, so should we, as led by the Spirit.

Don't be surprised at this, for it is the Bible truth. Jesus said,

> **Think not that I am come to send peace on earth: I came not to send peace, but a sword. For I am come to set a man at variance against his father, and the daughter against her mother, and the daughter in law against her mother in law. And a man's foes shall be they of his own household** (Matthew 10:34-36).

This may sound difficult, but it is the pathway to the power of God. When we begin to love righteousness and hate iniquity as Jesus did, the attitude of our heart will change concerning the rejection of the gospel. We will still have compassion for the heathen and we will never show anger, but our love of the holiness of God will supersede the tendency to cower and coddle to sinners. And it should supersede even our natural tendency toward careless family members that Jesus called "foes of (our) own household." We will feel as God feels: He has great mercy, but He also obeys his laws of choice and spiritual attitude of the new covenant. Here is Paul's reaction when the Jews rejected him:

> **Then Paul and Barnabas waxed bold, and said, It was necessary that the word of God should first have been spoken to you: but seeing ye put it from you, and judge yourselves unworthy of everlasting life, lo, we turn to the Gentiles** (Acts 13:46).

And at Corinth with both Jews and Greeks present, "And when they opposed themselves, and blasphemed, he shook his raiment, and said unto them, *Your blood be upon your own heads; I am clean: from henceforth I will go unto the Gentiles*" (Acts 18:6). It seems that Paul said this twice to different groups of Jews, as if he was willing to give Israel a second chance. We should always watch for God's second, or third, or next chance to have mercy on the stiffnecked. Cast them to God. Stop needing their intimate friendship so much. Stop swimming in the same pond as the fish. Fish don't catch fish. Fishermen do. Get out of the pond, depart, and wait for later.

16
The Grease Factory

One day a man visited his brother whom he hadn't seen in a very long time. This brother had designed and built a factory that made grease, so he proudly took his visiting brother on a tour of the manufacturing facility. He showed him the gigantic grease-making machine, all the conveyors, the bells and whistles, the gears and mechanisms, and all the grease that was in process—quite elaborate and impressive. After a couple of hours, the man noticed that something was missing. He asked his brother, "So, when do I get to see the finished product—the packaged grease, the pallets, the distribution warehouse—the money making part?" His brother hung his head in embarrassment and replied, "Well, that's the only problem. The machine that I've built requires so much grease to run that there isn't any grease left to package and send to people."

The Church must take heed. We cannot be found with such a huge "machine" of internal activity that we have no time, energy, or anointing to emphasize our duty to the lost. Our soul has only so much capacity. It cannot be consumed with just *anything*, or it won't have any stamina for the *vital* things. We have mastered a lot of things—our gatherings, our offering collecting, our stage dramas and videos, our music,

WITNESS PRINCIPLE 20

What Our Commission is *Not*

and our laser lights. We have mastered the Charismatic dance, the contemporary hop, the Pentecostal shake, and the Baptist hymnal. And then there's some doctrinal "creations" we're striving to master. But have we mastered the great commission of the Lord Jesus Christ—the art of personal evangelism?

Please allow me a chapter to convey some perspective, because at some point in your walk with God, you'll certainly encounter various "seemingly spiritual" efforts that begin to interfere with your gospel priorities. It all boils down to emphasis. If we fail to emphasize the *right* things, we get entangled in "other things." Anytime someone loses sight of the goal, the purpose, or the finish line, their course is detoured elsewhere. And we really can't afford that. Only with *correct* spiritual perspective can we properly distribute the gospel power of God. Only the *absolute truth* can keep us free and happy. I'm trying to inspire us all back to New Testament scripture—back toward the one assignment given by Jesus—the call of the Christian. I'm all for people having interests and hobbies in whatever they like. So, I'm not touching what you do in your spare time. But if we're not careful, personal interests can get elevated into convictions that were never commanded by the Lord Jesus. And then they begin to take valuable time, money, and attention away from our gospel-spreading efforts.

This happens to the Church quite often with some of the misleading teachings that pop up here and there, distracting innocent believers. Whether it's some far-fetched-false-prophetic-superstitious vision or over-emphasis on some non-

New-Testament subject, people get lured into excitement about something other than the "boring old" great commission. For example, many Christians are being told that "the biggest thing God is doing right now is with Israel. Just look at the Middle East—it's all about that." No, it's not. It's still all *and only* about Jesus Christ. From that, there's an occasional push to get the Church to learn Jewish customs and embrace all the Jewish traditions, as if becoming more Jewish will improve our Christ-likeness. And they do it in the name of promoting "pro-Semitism" rather than "anti." Not fair. True Christians are pro-everybody. And no non-Jew was ever commanded by the Lord to become more Jewish. We're children of Abraham by faith alone, and that's all it takes. (When *unsaved* Jewish rabbis are allowed to preach on Christian television stations, clearly someone has lost their way.) Nothing has changed since the Son of God rose from the dead and gave us our commission. It's still all about Him and all about making New Testament, blood–bought disciples. God is only concerned right now with turning unbelievers (of every race) into believers and in filling believers with His Spirit and His Word. And there is absolutely no instruction given to the Church to do anything specific for Israel or Jerusalem except preach the gospel there (I realize King David told the Israelites to "pray for the peace of Jerusalem." But I'm emphasizing that Jesus gave no such command to the New Testament Church). God has an end time plan for Israel, and certainly we acknowledge the signs of the times. But when it comes to unbelieving Israelites, if we're not going straight at them to turn them to Christ (and shaking the dust if they reject us), we've gone soft and wrong.

It's similar with other so called "causes" that run crosswise to the pure gospel. For example, fighting over the ten commandment monuments outside courthouses, arguing over the words "Merry Christmas", and filing lawsuits so we can keep baby Jesus manger scenes everywhere is quite confusing. On one hand, it seems noble because this sin-infected secular world is so wrong. But on the other hand, we must be careful, because political battlefronts are not our gospel commission. I appreciate those who feel called (by vocation) into the government arena to protect the high standard of our constitutional rights and to propagate what is right. I would agree that being salt and light to the world includes influencing it in every way we can, including politically if we are called there. But even more than that, our salt and light is for the individual sinner next to us, so they can understand Jesus Christ, glorify God, and be saved. As the Body of Christ, the state of the nation is not our top priority. The state of the Kingdom is. In the Christian's mind, the top problems we face should not be nation problems of bad government, but Kingdom problems of Satan darkening and destroying the people we're trying to save. Our Kingdom purposes should stir us up more than Fox News does. When I speak of being a "world-changer", I am *not* referring to taking over local or national governments, but rather turning the next person, and the next, to Jesus Christ, and living with holy power.

I would certainly prefer a righteous government. I am passionate about the difficulties our country and our world faces. And I am as dissatisfied as anyone with a country that is split 50-50 down the middle politically and morally. I am a stalwart Bible conservative, and I am concerned about the heathen spiral our country seems to be in. But because I am a Christian, I must be *more* concerned with the *individuals* who are in that spiral and headed to hell. Even during an election year, our heart should beat, not for turning blue states to red, but for turning sinners to Christ. The atmosphere of a nation comes from its people. If we want any sort of real morality in the land, we'll need to target the *spirit* of man. Getting people saved and righteous on the *inside first* is what Jesus died for. And saying "Merry Christmas" during December certainly doesn't save anybody. The problem is not the president or his policies. It is the *people*. The problem is not if the *president* approves of same sex marriage. The problem is when almost *half of the population* approves of same sex marriage! The answers for the country will never be found in legislating politics. We can certainly write our congressman. We can vote. And we can pray for those in authority and stop spiritual attacks against the country as the Lord directs us. But the lasting answers are found in the spiritual revival of *individuals*.

We must admit that right now, the Lord Jesus has not authorized Theocracy—the divine, totalitarian government ruled by the law of God. Deep down, that's what we believers are really wanting. And that's why we get so frustrated when things don't go our way politically. Right now, it is very difficult for us to mandate righteous rule in the country (or the world) because the Lord has not yet empowered us for that. Authority for world-wide Theocracy doesn't come until the millennial reign of Christ. Most of the early Jews entirely missed the Messiah for doing that—for thinking it was time to take over with Godly law and rise to the top with natural ruler-ship. But *we* can't fall for it, or we'll remain distracted, frustrated, and stuck with an attitude of animosity toward people rather than compassion. We must acknowledge that God *could* have given us natural ruler-ship as well as spiritual ruler-ship at the first coming of Christ, but He didn't. He only authorized His disciples on the spiritual side. We must accept God's will in the matter—that He chose *not* to pursue righteous *legislating*, but rather to pursue the *hearts* of men.

This perspective was challenging even for the early disciples. Right in the middle of Jesus giving them His great final words of Holy Spirit promise "...you shall be baptized with the

Holy Spirit not many days from now", they were still concerned about their country, "Lord, will you at this time restore the kingdom to Israel?" Their carnal minds were set on natural coup d'etat, but Jesus side-stepped the question and redirected them to the main purpose.

> **It is not for you to know times or seasons which the Father has put in His own authority. But you shall receive power when the Holy Spirit has come upon you; and you shall be witnesses to Me…** (Acts 1:5-8).

Nothing has changed since that day, except that the Holy Spirit fell and filled those disciples, who never again emphasized the state of their nation nor picketed for freedom of speech. And as a result, they ignited Kingdom revival right under the nose of the oppressive Roman government.

The trumpet call from heaven was never "save your government", but "save souls." Regardless of what some might be saying, *since the cross,* God is *not* dealing with *nations* on a national level (not even America), but with *individuals* on a personal level. Salvation and righteousness through Jesus Christ is presented to *people,* not to countries. And that's why, as inspiring as all the teaching on "Christian" politics can be, it never gets enough traction to create lasting results. Logic seems to tell us that 'God's will' must certainly be to get Christians into governments around the world. But let's keep it real. The only real command God has given us about government leaders is to pray for them so that we Christians can continue our lives and our gospel work in peace. And admit that according to New Testament scripture and emphasis, God wants to pour His Spirit on people ("…I will pour out of my Spirit on all flesh…") more than He wants to win an election or change a law. And that deserves our full attention.

My point is that if we're going to fight about something, let's fight the real fight. Forget the ten commandments in the schools. Let's be bold and post John 3:16 in the schools. If we're going to write God's commandments anywhere, let's make it the top two *New Testament* commandments. If we're going to impact a graduation ceremony, let's give people a 30 second salvation speech rather than only add Jesus' name to the end of our prayer. And let's tell the gospel to people at the shopping malls rather than proudly toot our "Merry Christmas" to prove we're more spiritual than the "Happy Holidays" people. We've wasted much thought and breath about political frustrations, and not enough thought and breath on personally sharing the love and power of God with the lost person next to us. If we're rallying for real solutions, let's make it for *revival in the land.* Maybe we need to start with revival *in us.* If we're praying intensely for something, let's make it for the salvation of our people. I believe that the reason that radical government changes occur (i.e. the crumbling of the Berlin Wall, or the fall of Communism), is because people are praying for the salvation of souls, and not because people are praying for specific government policies (clearly, policy praying hasn't been working for us). If we do our part for the Kingdom, God will do His part for our family, our city, and our nation. But then again, a changed, conservative nation should not be our goal, but rather a by-product of our Kingdom goal—*preach the gospel and save another soul so God's Spirit can flood into their life.*

I know this sounds a bit different than traditional "Christian–speak", but it's more Biblical and more real. I like real Christianity. I like real gospel power and real honor of Jesus' commands—the ones in the Bible. Fighting for any cause other than the one Jesus Christ commissioned will always either lead to corruption, or it will lead to distracted Christians who don't compassionately share the gospel of Jesus Christ with any sinner for years. Why does this happen? It happens because it's much easier to rally around a natural political position or cultural stance than it is to stay on our toes spiritually and go after the souls of people. It's much easier to focus on outside distractions than it is to keep oneself on fire for God and *light it up* for every person we meet.

Know the purpose of the cross. Know *your* purpose as a Christian. God has always had great purpose planned for us. He has always wanted a bigger family. He made Adam and Eve and gave them their commission, "Make babies." After the flood, He gave Noah his commission, "Make babies." Now, He commissions believers to, "Make more believers. Give me more family." It's what God has always wanted.

17
Happy Are the Soul-Winners

It's more blessed to give than to receive (Acts 20:35).

The happiest people are always the ones who are giving out, sharing their life with others. John G. Lake said that a person's physical health follows their spiritual health. If a person's *body* is sick, it's a result of a *spirit* that is sick, weak, or frail. He went on to say that there were three key ingredients to a healthy spirit: 1) Feed on the Word of God daily. 2) Have a consistent communion with the Holy Spirit—a healthy prayer life. And, 3) Have a fresh testimony on your lips at all times to others—of Christ, who He is to you, what He has done for you, what He will do for another.

It is important for us to spend time hearing great teaching and preaching, praising, worshiping, and studying our Bibles. But we must not stop there. We must *let out* what we have *put in*. If we only receive this great gospel in our hearts but don't share it, we will stagnate. We will become like the Dead Sea. It is dead because it receives water from the river Jordan, but it has no rivers leaving it. All the salt and minerals are deposited into it, but they never leave. So it stagnates, contaminates itself, and the life that was in it isn't living anymore.

Watchman Nee, a great apostle to China in the twentieth century, said this,

> **"But let me say that the channel of life has two ends: One end is open toward the Holy Spirit; but the other end is open toward men. The water of life will not flow if only the end toward the Lord is open. The other end, the end toward the world must be open too for there to be any flowing. The reason many do not have power before God is due to their either being closed on the end toward the Lord or on the end toward sinners. China can still be won to Christ if we open our hearts to men."**

He said people *have no power* because they are closed somewhere. I say that they are also *not happy* for the same reason.

WITNESS PRINCIPLE 21

Don't Be the Dead Sea

It's a vicious cycle. If we're not spiritually healthy, we won't want to help others. If we are depressed, the last thing we want to do is be around anybody. And we certainly don't feel any ability to bless, help, or witness for God. But conversely, if we *don't* spend time helping others, we will weaken in fervor, get depressed, and remain spiritually feeble. And around we go, spiraling downward into lethargy and into spiritual sleep, unable to do anything good or feel anything joyful.

It is the same with sin. If we are in sin, the last thing we feel like doing is sharing the love of God. If we are in sin, our guilt makes us feel like a hypocrite, so what good is it for us to share our faith with someone else? But conversely, if we *don't* consistently share our faith, we remain weak and sickly in our soul and are more prone to sin. We feel stuck in the sin-no-witnessing cycle, and down we go.

But, there is hope! I have found that there is a way out. The way out of the quagmire of depression is to go share your faith with someone else. The quickest way out of sin is to go win a soul. Go share your life, go give, go serve someone else, and the blessing will come from the Lord. You'll feel good and happy for at least a little while. And for a little while, you didn't sin. For a little while, you were forced to smile. You interrupted the devil's depression script inside your mind and did something holy. And it felt good. Now, you could just go back to the old way of depression and sin. Or, you could just do another giving, serving, witnessing thing and double your happy time. Do it back to back, and feel good twice as long. I have observed that making a commitment to witness consistently will, by its very nature, also help us commit to getting out of sin. When we take a step of faith to do what is right and of God, we enter the "boxing match" with our difficulty, and the fight begins. But at least it's better than forfeiting to sin and depression as they dance around an empty ring, waving their gloves at our face in victory. You won't feel like doing it, I assure you. Our flesh would much rather lay around the couch of despair than fight something or go be around somebody. But that's what this holy fight of faith is all about. We walk by faith, not by sight or feeling. We please God this way. And we win.

We are all happier when we are giving what we've got, whether time, effort, money, or the Word we know. For example, the senior pastor of a church tends to be happier than the associate pastor. I've seen it many times. Why? Because the senior pastor usually does more of the preaching. He is consistently filling up and giving out, while the associate fills up a lot more than he gives out. Even the children's pastor is sometimes happier than the associate pastor because the children's pastor is teaching every week. Preachers, take note of this, and help to relieve the associates. Associates, *and pastor's spouses,* find a way to give out. Find a small group to teach. Lead an outreach. Teach a Bible study. And make a commitment to a lifestyle of personal witnessing. You don't need the pulpit to be happy. Just find an outlet to give what you've got. I've done this, and it works. I was an associate in one church and a leader in another, and never did I ever get stuck and stagnate, waiting for the pulpit to open up. Why? Because I had so much fun and contentment sharing my faith with anyone who would listen (and some who wouldn't). The scripture says to be content in whatever state you are in. And I agree. But I assure you, none of us will ever be spiritually content if we are not actively sharing Christ with others.

I realize that if you've never done this, "fun" is the last word you would use to describe it. But "getting into" something only requires a little time and attention. Anything you give your attention to will eventually rise to the forefront of your priorities. And then you can experience the satisfaction and the divine glory of it.

One notable Proverb is, "As arrows are in the hand of a mighty man; so are children of the youth. Happy is the man that has his quiver full of them" (Psalm 127:4-5). This scripture is referring to a father having many children. But how can it be so certain he is happy? He is happy because he knows he is multiplying himself. The Christian is also happy if he is multiplying himself spiritually. And he is secretly sad if not.

"It is the only happy life to live for the salvation of souls."

—D. L. Moody

18
BOLDNESS

What is boldness? It is the decision to act on what is right regardless of what we fear. It is similar to courage, which is a power or strength to meet a scary circumstance head on because there is a need.

Watchman Nee told this story,

> "Beloved," he began, "what I tell you now truly happened. A young man named Todd was led to Christ by a wise couple from a church in his neighborhood. He had been a rebellious youth, but on the day that he was saved, he asked the couple what he should do to show his obedience to the Lord. Over tea in their home, they told him that the gospel would never make inroads in their town until a certain battalion commander was converted. Young Todd asked who this Commander Deeds was. They said that he was a retired military man over sixty years of age who thought all Christians were hypocrites and who cursed and beat any Christian who dared to preach the gospel to him or even to pass by his house. He kept a pistol at home and threatened to open fire on anyone who preached to him.
>
> Having heard this, Todd immediately prayed, "O Lord, You have shown grace to me. This is the first day of my

salvation. I will go and witness to him." Before tea was finished, and less than two hours after his own salvation, he was on his way to the commander's house. Fearing for his life, the couple begged him not to go. The commander's anger grew fiercer by the day, they told him, but Todd would not change his mind. He arrived at the house and knocked on the door. The commander answered with a rod in his hand and snarled, "What do you want, boy?" Todd asked if he could come in, and for some reason the hostile man allowed him entrance. The boy wasted no words. "I pray that you will accept the Lord Jesus as your Savior!" he blurted out. The commander raised his rod in the air to intimidate the youth, then shouted, "I suppose you're new around here, so this time I will pardon you; no one talks to me about Jesus, but this time I will not beat you. Now consider yourself fortunate and get out of here quickly!" Though he knew his life was in danger, Todd refused to leave. "I beg you to believe on the Lord Jesus," he said. The commander was furious. He went upstairs and came down with his pistol. "Go, or I will shoot you now," he threatened. Todd answered, "I have come to ask you to believe in the Lord Jesus. If you want to shoot me, go ahead. But before you do, let me pray for you." He knelt before the commander and prayed, "O God, here is a man who does not know You. Please save him!" he cried out. "Have mercy on the commander." Young Todd prayed like this for several minutes before he heard a sigh, then the sound of the pistol being laid aside. Soon the commander knelt down beside him and, after a moment of weeping, prayed, "O God, have mercy on Commander Deeds."

The commander was saved at that instant, and after praying some more, he rose and took the hand of his young friend, saying, "I have heard the gospel all my life, but today I have seen the gospel for the first time." On the following Lord's Day, Commander Deeds went to the

church to worship. And before he died, he led several dozen people to the Lord."

Every eye in the auditorium was on Watchman; the audience was deeply moved by his story. "Beloved," he said, "there are two big days in the life of the believer: the day on which he believes in the Lord, and every day after that when he leads someone to faith in Christ. This is my challenge to you. Witness to at least one person a day. Witness to whomever you meet" (Laurent, p. 100-103).

Boldness is not some mystical thing that must be prayed for and sought after. It is simply a belief that God actually said these things, and that we must do these things. Boldness is *sold-out obedience.* Boldness comes when you're one hundred percent committed to a thing. Boldness comes by faith—by knowing that God will do what He said, "that with all boldness they may speak Your word, by stretching forth Your hand to heal, and that signs and wonders may be done through the name of Your holy Servant Jesus" (Acts 4:29,30). If you need to pray about it, fine. But afterwards, don't wait for some feeling of boldness. Don't wait, just go. Boldness comes by believing that God will back you up by healing the sick, working miracles, and convincing of sin—not by just asking, "God, give me boldness." And eventually, you'll even feel a bit bolder.

> **WITNESS PRINCIPLE 22**
>
> Boldness Comes Only After You're Sold-Out

Courage and boldness are traits of Spirit-filled people. If we're maintaining a Spirit-filled life, we'll be more in tune with God than natural threats. We will more easily remember that we are not alone—that "greater is He that is in me, than he that is in the world" (1 John 4:4). We've ministered in some of the scariest places in America—some of the worst, gang-ridden, drug centers of downtown areas in America. But because we knew the Lord was with us, we took no precaution for our own lives. People sometimes heard of where we were headed and felt obligated to warn us of the danger, but it was not needed. They just had forgotten what God said, "The angel of the Lord encamps all around those who fear Him, and delivers them" (Psalm 34:7). But only Spirit-filled people remember that. Only Spirit-filled people actually believe that and live that. When you're close to the Spirit, He reminds you that the Lord is near and that there is nothing to fear. And only when we believe it will He do it. No danger gets to threaten me. No thug gets to kill me. And no uncommon persecution gets to destroy me (unless, of course, I've lived all my days out and completed all the life and ministry God has called me to, and only if God has revealed to me ahead of time what will happen, like he did with Paul and Peter).

It is always an amazing experience to see the peace and love that blankets an area when we believers venture into it with the gospel. Hardened gangsters get humbled and nice, thanking us for coming, even if they didn't receive Christ. And violence turns off. During my five summers with R.W. Schambach's tent crusades, we would set up right in the middle of some of the darkest areas of the most crime-ridden cities, blast the gospel preaching and music from 7:00 p.m. until midnight sometimes, and walk the streets witnessing during the daytime. And the response was this: salvations and deliverance for multitudes, and blanketing peace in the community. Community officials always admitted that they had fewer domestic complaints and sometimes zero crime during the two weeks we were there. That is the Lord. And that is what Spirit-filled believers can expect. So stay full, and be bold.

19

CANCER AND BUDDHISM—GONE!

For I will not dare to speak of any of those things which Christ has not accomplished through me, to make the Gentiles obedient, *in word and deed…in mighty signs and wonders, by the power of the Spirit of God*; so that from Jerusalem, and round about to Illyricum, *I have fully preached the gospel of Christ* (Romans 15:18-19).

We are commonly aware that the gospel includes the preaching of the Word. But notice that Paul said in order to 'fully preach' the gospel, the deeds (*through mighty signs and wonders, by the power…*) are also necessary. It is still true today.

In my second year of walking with God, I frequented a haircut salon in the same strip mall where my church was. The haircutter was a Vietnamese lady who spoke very broken English. I consistently shared Christ with her as best I could, and even gave her a gospel tract in Vietnamese. But she was still very tied to her family religion—Buddhism. One day, I noticed she was very sad, so I asked about it. She revealed to me that she had been diagnosed with breast cancer, and she was very scared. I told her Jesus would heal her if she would let Him, and she allowed me to lay hands on her. I cursed and rejected the cancer in the name of Jesus.

A couple weeks later, she came excitedly running to find me at the church during work hours—no more cancer! She had gone back to the doctor, and he couldn't find any trace of it. Praise the Lord. As the next weeks went by, I continued trying to lead her to receive Jesus each time she cut my hair, but with the language barrier and all, I kept hitting a wall.

Finally, the Lord gave me an idea (howbeit, a very obvious one). I had been involved with a weekly pastors' prayer meeting for a while, and one of the guys that I had become acquainted with was a Vietnamese Methodist pastor from a church down the street. I picked him up one day and asked him to come with me to speak to this lady. We sat with her for about 30 minutes, and he translated what I said to her about salvation through Jesus Christ. At one point, she began to cry and tearfully explained her dilemma. If she were to accept Jesus Christ, she would be rejecting Buddha, and by doing so, rejecting her family. She said they would disown her if she became a Christian. But, then it happened. The Holy Spirit must have completed His work, because she stopped crying in a moment and emphatically made her life-long decision for Jesus. And she was born again. She was totally transformed and soon began attending that Vietnamese Methodist church. She even came to our church once to give God glory. These are the words she said as she stood up to testify in her broken English, "Jesus love me. He heal me from cancer."

WITNESS PRINCIPLE 23

Healing Goes with Preaching

I haven't seen her in a long time, but I know that even five years later, she was still attending that Vietnamese Methodist church and serving God.

It is absolutely clear from the scriptures that the Lord Jesus intended the preaching of the gospel to also include the healing of sick people and the casting out of demons. Don't let any preacher or any false teaching tell you otherwise. Miracles and healing can be very misunderstood because of the element of faith that is required, but that doesn't negate the fact of the spirit realm and the power of God for those who believe it. The salvation of God through Jesus Christ includes deliverance and healing from everything—spirit, soul, and body. And many times, the physical touch of God is the dinner bell for salvation. Experiencing God's goodness is often necessary to awaken a desire for God.

> And when he had called unto him his twelve disciples, he *gave them power against unclean spirits, to cast them out, and to heal all manner of sickness and all manner of disease* (Matthew 10:1).

> And he ordained twelve, that they should be with him, and that he might send them forth to preach, *And to have power to heal sicknesses, and to cast out devils* (Mark 3:14,15).

> And he called unto him the twelve, and began to send them forth by two and two; *and gave them power over unclean spirits*...And they went out, and preached that men should repent, and *they cast out many devils, and anointed with oil many that were sick, and healed them* (Mark 6:7,12,13).

> Then he called his twelve disciples together, and *gave them power and authority* over all devils, and to cure diseases. And he sent them to preach the kingdom of God, *and to heal the sick*...And they departed and went

> through the towns, preaching the gospel, *and healing everywhere* (Luke 9:1,2).
>
> Go ye into all the world, and preach the gospel to every creature. He that believeth and is baptized shall be saved…And *these signs shall follow them that believe*; in my name shall they *cast out devils*; they shall speak with new tongues…they shall *lay hands on the sick and they shall recover*…And they went forth, and preached everywhere, the Lord working with them, and confirming the word *with signs following* (Mark 16:15-17).
>
> And that repentance and remission of sins should be preached in his name…And, behold, I send the promise of my Father upon you: But tarry ye in the city of Jerusalem, until ye be *endued with power from on high* (Luke 24:47,49).

It is no mistake. Each time Jesus sends His disciples out with a commission, He gives them power to heal plus a command to do it. So, be bold to obey Jesus. He is waiting to work with *you.*

Another time I was on the front porch of a pastor friend's house speaking with his teenagers. One of their teenage friends showed up, and I turned to them and asked out loud, "Is your friend saved? Is he a Christian?" As they shrugged, I turned to the boy and asked him personally. He said that he hadn't been to church in a long time, since his mother died, and he didn't know anything about being saved. I shared the message of Christ with him and led him to confess Jesus as his Lord. He was saved. But then I had an urge to ask him if there was anything else he needed God to do for him—any sickness or pain or anything else. He explained that his knee had been injured two years prior, and that it still hurt him when he jumped and ran. I touched him and commanded his knee to be healed and for the pain to go. And the power of God gently touched him. I then told him to do something he couldn't do before, and he started jumping up and down with a big smile on his face. The pain was gone and he was healed! Praise the Lord Jesus Christ.

I learned that the moment a person receives Christ is sometimes the best moment to offer the healing power of God. Jesus died to save us from sin and also from sickness (1 Peter 2:24), so why not offer them together? The instant that a person confesses Christ, the Holy Spirit comes into the person. At that moment, they are closer to God's power than ever before, so it's a good time to help them receive that power for healing.

And look at this: if we examine the word 'witness', according to the dictionary, a witness is one who has known or seen something and can give proof to its truth. So what did we see? What testimony do we have of anything? Notice what the early Church was a witness of.

> **...must one be ordained to be a *witness with us of his resurrection*** (Acts 1:22).
>
> **This Jesus hath *God raised up,* whereof we all are witnesses** (Acts 2:32).
>
> **And killed the Prince of life, *whom God hath raised from the dead*; whereof we are witnesses** (Acts 3:15).
>
> **And with great power gave the *apostles witness of the resurrection* of the Lord Jesus...** (Acts 4:33).

The apostles gave witness of His resurrection—not of His death. Of course the death is part of it, for how can one be resurrected if He never died? But "And if Christ be not raised, your faith is vain; ye are yet in your sins" (1 Corinthians 15:17). Many martyrs have died, but only Christ has been raised up! The resurrection carries with it the miracle working power.

So what have you seen? Did you see the resurrection? No. The first twelve apostles were eye-witnesses, but we are not. We saw nothing. But guess who did see it? The Holy Spirit. He actually performed it. And He lives in *us.* So when we speak of the resurrection, we can do it with authority. And we can prove it with power. We can heal the sick (and we should); we can cast out devils (and we should); and we can expect other gifts of the Spirit to cause people to listen. We are witnesses of the life-changing power of the Spirit *within,* and of the healing power of the Spirit *upon.* He is in us and with us.

20
Are You Serving Two Masters?

Aside from fear, from not enough time, from being distracted, and from being untrained, what else makes it so hard for so many Christians to form a habit of witnessing? The love of money. Not money itself, but "the love of money is the root of all kinds of evil" (1 Timothy 6:10). Yes, the root of all evil even touches your Christian soul-winning efforts. Now bear with me here, so I can explain the spiritual significance of this. If you're already thinking about skipping this chapter, then you most definitely need to read it. The love of money is one of those complex subjects, like 'pride'. Both pride and the love of money are hard to dissect because their very nature repels the hearing of truth. Here is the basic principle: when the kingdom of God is top priority in a person's life, spiritual things are easy. Bible reading is a delight, daily praying is easy, and spreading the

> **Witness Principle 24**
>
> The Love of Money Will Stifle You

gospel to the next person is on the forefront of the believer's mind. If the believer is still stuck in the love of money, then money secretly remains the top priority of his consciousness and fights day and night against the kingdom work he desires to do. Money is part of life. And being successful and prosperous is part of this great covenant with God through Christ. But we can't fall into the trap of pursuing it, or it will evade us and deter us. Jesus said, "...he who loses his life for my sake will find it" (Matthew 10:39). And, "No servant can serve two masters; for either he will hate the one and love the other, or else he will be loyal to the one and despise the other. You cannot serve God and mammon" (Luke 16:13). Emphasizing the wrong priority will cause us to despise the right one.

Let me define the love of money just briefly because there are many misconceptions and shallow understandings of it. First, the love of money can reside in a rich person or a poor person. Some have cast off the thought of it saying, "Well, I know I don't love money because I don't have any to love." That is a weak argument. Actually, the most intense love for money can be in the person who has none. They yearn for it day and night. They stress over it at home and work. They grudge against the world for their not having it. They mistakenly think that if they had some more money, their life would be comforted. They feel they got the short end of the stick. They feel that just a little more money would solve their problems. They work a little harder. They push aside family a little to make an extra buck. They neglect church a little because their focus is on "making ends meet." They neglect their serving at church. They neglect their Christian duty to witness outside church. They're too depressed to do anything holy and good. They serve the almighty dollar. Money has taken the place of God.

God should be our comfort. God should be our problem solver. God should be our focus. When He is, then all things are added to us (Matthew 6:33). When He isn't, all things suffer—our finances, our spiritual growth, and our witnessing—because our focus is off. We are stuck in self-preservation mode. We have been deceived by selfishness. We have been deceived by the *deceitfulness of riches.* And we will rarely witness. Leading someone else to Jesus becomes a second rate activity compared to our most pressing need of earning income. And then we rationalize it with, "I've got to take care of my family. I'm only doing it for them." Yes, we should work, and we should care for our family. But when work is done, we should be serving God in our spare time. If our priorities are off, then winning souls will seem insignificant compared to the rest of life, and we won't do it. Sharing our faith will feel like an interruption that we can't afford. You know, "we're so busy and all, that all those sinners will just have to find God on their own, like me, you know, I searched for God and found Him on my own." (No you didn't, someone else planted some seed in you somewhere, sometime.) I've seen many good Christians learn of our covenant of prosperity but get deceived and sidetracked into seeking more money, over-emphasizing more money, and missing the true blessing of God because of it. The secret is: be in the will of God, do the will of God, seek first His kingdom, and money will come without you making a big deal about it.

Then on the other hand, when the bank account gets full and things feel comfortable, the rich and full must be warned not to trust in those riches. We can, and should, have plenty of money because of our covenant with God. But money shouldn't "have" us. Lots of money can become our god just as easily as no money. Money can solve natural problems and be relied upon in many situations. That can cause us to forget that God is our partner. He is our helper. He is the one we should lean on. We must keep our priorities straight and serve God with highest priority—both inside church where the saints gather and outside church where the sinners are. High-powered executives can be great Christians, but they'll need to guard themselves from the intense pressures of so much responsibility and stay free in spirit to serve God. We've watched many people come to church needing a job but eager to serve the Lord and learn the Word. We pray for them to get a job, we teach them that God has promised to care for them and supply their need, and we show them how to trust God. And they are hopeful and enthused about this kingdom. Next, God comes through for them, they get a great job that pays real money, and we never see them again. When we contact the lost sheep, we frequently hear, "But I just want you to know that even though I don't come to church anymore, I still pray every day." How embarrassing.

Even preachers have to be careful when things get comfortable. Don't slow down, don't forget your gift to the Church, and don't forget your personal Christian duty. Pastors sometimes feel such great responsibility for so many people in the congregation that "messing with someone outside the church" seems too much. It should not be so.

At our church, I recently taught a certain series called 'Seven Links in the Prosperity Chain'. In it, I addressed the love of money and how self-seeking is the roadblock to our spiritual life. At the time, I didn't mention anything about witnessing. But a young man in our church had a great revelation that week that changed his life. He was driving down the street a couple days after the message on Sunday, and he saw a homeless man that he thought he ought to talk to. But as he considered the hassle that it would be, and as he tried to reason himself out of it, the Spirit rose up within him. All at once, the Lord showed him how his secret inward stress and selfish pursuit of more money was the sole reason he wasn't bold to share Christ with others. A couple of weeks prior, he had even come up to the altar for me to pray that he would have more boldness to witness, but had still seen no change. He stopped his car and ran to talk to the homeless man. And ever since then, he has been free and bold to lead others to Jesus—I mean radical for Jesus at his work, in his personal life, and even with strangers. And he's been growing substantially in the scriptures. Why is that? Because he got free from himself. The good thing is that this young man realized it early.

There's no greater freedom that when a man gets freed from *himself.* And striving for money can, many times, be the biggest part of self, regardless of how much you have or don't have, and regardless of how much you act like money doesn't matter. It does matter. It matters for natural life, it matters for spiritual life, it matters how you think of it, and it matters what place you give it. If we're not "faithful with unrighteous mammon, who can trust to us the *true riches*" (Luke 16:11). What are the true riches? Everything of the kingdom, everything of God, and souls.

PART 2
STRATEGY, MECHANICS, THEOLOGY

21
Three Men. Three Buildings. One Purpose.

God always has a purpose for everything He does. And it is no different with the great commission. The purpose of the great commission culminates in eternity with God for believers, but it actually is even larger in scope than that. God is building something. He is building something for Himself, and just like always, He's chosen people to get it done. If we notice real closely in the Bible, we find three men who were given similar building projects. I'm not speaking of Noah and the ark, but rather three men who were commissioned to build temples for God. Each project required the same ingredients for success: a holy purpose, a blueprint, an offering, and skillful, obedient laborers.

The First Builder

The first builder is Moses. The first building is the tabernacle—the mobile sanctuary for the Israelites' wilderness journey. The purpose for this portable tabernacle? To provide a place for God to meet with man. "And let them make me a sanctuary; *that I may dwell among them...* And there I will meet with thee" (Exodus 25:8, 22). The blueprint contained an elaborate design detail, dictated by God, "According to all that I show you...*the pattern* of the tabernacle...." (Verse 9). The building required money and materials, which was to come from the people. "Speak to the children of Israel, that they *bring Me an offering.* From everyone who gives it willingly with his heart..." (Exodus 25:2).

And finally, to put it all together, he needed workers—skilled ones.

> **I have called by name Bezaleel...And I have filled him with the spirit of God, in wisdom, and in understanding, and in knowledge, and in all manner of workmanship, To devise cunning works, to work in gold, and in silver, and in brass, and in cutting of stones, to set them, and in carving of timber, to work in all manner of workmanship. And I, behold, I have given with him Aholiab, ...and in the hearts of all that are wise hearted I have put wisdom, that they may make all that I have commanded thee** (Exodus 31:2-6).

The Second Builder

The second builder is Solomon. The second building is the temple in Jerusalem, made of hewn stones from the mountains.

> **And he said unto me, Solomon thy son, he shall build my house and my courts...for the Lord hath chosen thee to build an house for the sanctuary: be strong, and do it** (1 Chronicles 28:6, 10-12).

Again, the purpose was clear. It was not a house for man, but a house for the Lord to dwell in.

> **...the work is great: for *the palace is not for man, but for the Lord God*...and Solomon determined to build an house for the *name of the Lord*, and *an house for his kingdom*** (1 Chronicles 29:1; 2 Chronicles 2:1).

The blueprint, the pattern of the temple, was given by God to David.

> **Then David gave to Solomon his son the pattern of the porch...And the pattern of all that he had by the spirit...** (1 Chronicles 28:11-12).

Next, the offering was given willingly by the people.

> **Then the chief of the fathers and princes of the tribes of Israel, and the captains of thousands and of hundreds, with the rulers of the king's work, offered willingly, And gave for the service of the house of God of gold five thousand talents...Then the people rejoiced, for that they offered willingly, because with perfect heart they *offered willingly to the Lord*...** (1 Chronicles 29:6-9).

Then the skillful laborers arrived and were given their assignments.

> **And, behold, the courses of the priests and the Levites, even they shall be with thee for all the service of the house of God: and there shall be with thee for all manner of workmanship every willing skilful man..." "And Solomon told out threescore and ten thousand men to bear burdens, and fourscore thousand to hew in the mountain, and three thousand and six hundred to oversee them** (1 Chronicles 28:21; 2 Chronicles 2:2).

The Third Builder

Now here is where it gets interesting. Who is the third man commissioned to build God a house?

The Lord Jesus Christ.

> **Behold, the man whose name is *The Branch*...he shall *build the temple of the Lord*...and he shall bear the glory, and shall sit and rule upon his throne; and he shall be a priest upon his throne...** (Zechariah 6:12,13).

Notice, Jesus is also called 'The Branch' in Isaiah.

> **...there shall come forth a rod out of the stem of Jesse, and a *Branch* shall grow out of his roots: and the spirit of the Lord shall rest upon Him** (Isaiah 11:1).

Could it be? Is it possible that the plan and purpose of God is more intricate than getting people into heaven? Why would God have said Jesus was going to build a temple? And what is that temple?

One day I was preaching in a certain church in Jacksonville, Texas. In the church foyer, I noticed a little painting of a close-up of Jesus holding a shepherd's staff. Behind Him were several little sheep in a field. And it hit me—the painting was wrong! Jesus, by trade, was not a shepherd. He was a carpenter. Of course, I know He is called our Great Shepherd, and symbolically, we are the people of His pasture. But in the natural, He was *not* a sheep shepherd. He was a builder—a carpenter just like his earthly father, Joseph. His carpentry correlated to the spiritual "temple" He would build. His intent was to construct, to create, to build something. He understood things from a carpenter's view regarding foundation, structure, and precision. That's how He views our spiritual construction—requiring a solid foundation and focused development for our individual character and also for His positioning every member in their proper place in the Body.

WITNESS PRINCIPLE 25

We Are Building God a Temple

Notice the parallel in purpose. The old temples were built for God to have a place to dwell. And so is the temple that Jesus is building. *We* are built to give God a place to dwell.

> **But Solomon built him a house.** ***Howbeit the most High dwelleth not in temples made with hands...*** (Acts 7:47-48).
>
> **Know ye not that *ye are the temple of God,* and that the *Spirit of God dwelleth in you?*** (1 Corinthians 3:16).
>
> **And what agreement hath the temple of God with idols? For *ye are the temple of the living God;* as God hath said, *I will dwell in them, and walk in them,* and I will be their God, and they shall be my people** (2 Corinthians 6:16).

What for? God in man, just like He was in Jesus—destroying the works of the devil and spreading the glory of God into the earth. As individuals, Jesus is now our blueprint—the one we are to emulate. As the Church, our blueprint is the Book of Acts plus the epistles of the New Testament.

Notice the other parallels. Solomon's temple was built from perfectly hewn and carved stones. No mortar was used to stack and place the huge stones. They were precisely grooved together. So are Church members.

> **Ye are fellowcitizens with the saints, and of the household of God; and are built upon the foundation of the apostles and prophets, Jesus Christ himself being the chief corner**

> **stone. In whom all the building fitly framed together grows unto a holy temple in the Lord** (Ephesians 2:19-21).

Jesus is building *us*. And He's building us *to fit together*!

Jesus was called a "*Living Stone*" and that "You also, as living stones, are built up a spiritual house, a holy priesthood, to offer up spiritual sacrifices..." (1 Peter 2:4,5). The temple was to house God's presence and His name. Likewise, *we* house the name of Jesus. *We* house the glory of God. And *we* house the Spirit of God, who is God, Himself. Our goal is spiritual perfection as a holy Body.

Also, in this kingdom building, offerings are still given. Money is still needed to supply the materials for the work. The pattern of the Old Testament still applies—God requires His people to give of their precious substance, from their heart, willingly without pressure, to His holy purpose.

This Is Where You Come In

I set all this up to get here: this is where you come in. This is where we all must accept the call of the Christian. The temple requires stones. But the "stones" don't walk in by themselves. Someone must venture out to the mountains and with focused effort (sharing your faith), find ready rocks, carve them out (save souls out in the world), and make ugly stones perfect for the temple of God. This holy temple building requires laborers—skilled laborers. It requires the same laborers Solomon's temple required: hewers in the mountains, burden bearers to carry the stones, and overseers to train and direct. We can't *all* be overseers and temple tenders. When we're at church, we all have a certain position. But when we are out, we should be doing our stone cutting ministry. Everyone has a responsibility in getting those "lively stones" out of their lost world and placed into their spiritual home. And the temple will be built.

The Finished Work

What happens when the work is finished?

> **So Moses finished the work. Then a cloud covered the tent of the congregation, and the glory of the Lord filled the tabernacle** (Exodus 40:33-34).
>
> **Thus all the work that Solomon made for the house of the Lord was finished...then the house was filled with a cloud, even the house of the Lord; so that the priests could not stand to minister by reason of the cloud; for the glory of the Lord had filled the house of God** (2 Chronicles 5:1-14).

The glory of the Lord is our reward. And it's not a one-time glory that must wait for the entire Body of Christ to be finished. Certainly there will be the greatest glory that final day. But because each believer constitutes a temple of his own, the glory can fill us all, all the time. Alone, we can experience the glory of God. Together, we can experience the glory of God. Both alone and together we will help Jesus get His temple built. I know that Jesus said, "It is finished." But He was referring to His earthly ministry. He is certainly not finished with His new position as High Priest and Mediator. And He is not finished building His Church. Have you taken your place as a skilled laborer?

22
LAMB CHOPS OR LAW?

The command is, "...preach the gospel." The gospel is the *good news.* It's the goodness of God that leads men to repentance (Romans 2:4). The goal in ministering to people is to help them see that God's goodness is the remedy for all dissatisfaction in their life. Rather than target people's flesh indulgences as the issue, explain how the real issue is the spiritual void inside them. Flesh sins are not the problem, but rather a symptom—a feeble attempt to cure their spiritual emptiness and gain some comfort. Keep this in mind as you minister to people who are smoking, drinking, cussing, gambling in front of you, or to those who you have "inside" lifestyle information on, especially family members and co-workers. Never target the sin. You are not the "sin police", and forcing people to clean up on the outside never works. The smoking, drinking, cussing, gambling is not what is keeping them from God. It is their lack of desire for Him that keeps them from God. We can't clean the fish until we catch 'em. And we can't train the sinner until they've joined the Way.

I've heard of something called the "lamb chop theory", which is this: that if you try and take an old dirty bone away from a dog, telling him how bad it is for him, he'll growl at you. That's all he's got. But if you throw a nice, meaty lamb chop in front of him, he'll drop the old bone willingly to pick up the new, and you've gained a friend. Terry Mize, an apostle to the Church and missionary to the world, noted that missionaries have been killed for years because of doing this. In the name of the gospel, they go harp on what other religions are doing wrong, then get "bitten." In India, the Hindus have around 300 million false gods. And with all those gods over them, they are always feeling guilty for doing something wrong. Do they need someone to point that out? No, they need a lamb chop—the knowledge that they can be totally forgiven and accepted through Jesus Christ. Sin is not the sinner's problem. It is only the symptom. The problem is that the sinner isn't interested in God. They want their flesh pleasures and self-sufficient lifestyle more than the presence and person of the Spirit of God. And you can't fight that.

However, because we deal with so many different attitudes of people, we need to examine how our good news is given and received. Here is what I mean. If I just cut my finger, and I'm asking around for a bandage, and my wife pulls one out of her purse, "Here you go, Chas", then that is good news to me. But let's say that on another day, I've cut myself on a table and don't realize it. Someone offers me a bandage to wear but doesn't tell me why I need it. That is not good news to me—it is a useless gesture until they explain it. If I am on an airplane and someone offers me a parachute to wear for my trip, I will adamantly decline, as a parachute is not needed and would only make my journey more uncomfortable. But if that person informs me that the airplane is almost out of fuel and will soon crash, then the parachute is *great* news to me. And I will gladly bear a little bit of inconvenience to ensure a longer life. As a matter of fact, I would be trying to get a parachute for my family and for everyone else on board because of the new information.

So, you see, proper clarification may be required before someone perceives your news as good or not. To the *anxious sinner*—the one who feels conviction and desires to be accepted by God—to him we give only the good news of the Savior. But for the *unawakened sinner*—the one who feels no conviction toward God in any way, the one who is not desiring to know God, the one who feels no guilt for his Godless life and believes that no sin is really all that bad (except murder, of course)—to him, we must first give him some law—the bad news. He must be awakened to the reality of sin and its penalty of a future without God, without the love of God, and of eternal death. He needs to know he is "bleeding." He needs to know of the looming day of judgment—that his plane is going down! He needs to hear that eternal hell is the verdict for anyone without the Mediator. Once he recognizes his need for a Savior, he may be more open to your good news.

To the *one who is already awakened*, filled with the Spirit, filled with faith and love, to him it is okay to give him the whole instructional part of the Bible—the "Do this, avoid that, submit to God, resist the devil" part. Not orders and threats, but right things that please God. This is what a true Christian's feelings *demand*. He wants to please God, so telling him how is fine. His heart is crying out, "What can I do to honor and glorify God?" So giving him the wonderful instructions allows his heart to go forth to his spiritual responsibilities and New Testament requirements, of which there are many.

And finally, there are those who were once awakened to Christ but are now backslidden and lukewarm. These will be the people who "...profess that they know God, but in works they deny him, being abominable, and disobedient..." (Titus 1:16). What can you do? You can try anything you wish to help them. Expect the Holy Spirit to help them see the light. But if you recognize they are resisting you, halt your ministry to them immediately. Remember the principle? Only spend time on good ground—the good, honest, open hearted ones.

The point of the Lamb Chop Theory is to major on the solution of *relationship through Christ alone* rather than fall into the trap of law-mongering, scoffing at people's disobedience trying to force morality on them or to help them attain an appearance of spirituality without faith in their heart. Remember, it's the devil we're at war with—not people. And the only remedy for the devil and for people's iniquity is the goodness and grace of God through Christ and an individual's decision to accept Him.

So, on the note of lifestyle and attitude, don't let other people's sins get to you. It is their *nature* to sin. Sinners sin, just like dogs bark. It is in their spiritual DNA, until they get born again. So, don't go complaining about people's bad cussing habits, nor acting as if your sensitive Christian ears can't handle it, nor dictating the slang language rules when you're in the room. Just smile, let their own conscience do the convicting, and let the Holy Spirit do His work. If you do it right, eventually many people will decide all on their own to hide their sins from you out of respect. If people are belligerent about it, either smile real big and love them more, retaliate with a "praise the Lord Jesus Christ" every once in a while, or find a new room.

> **WITNESS PRINCIPLE 26**
>
> It's the Goodness of God That Turns People

I always make it a goal in front of people to never be moved by anything except the Lord. I have had strangers that I am talking to on the street blow cigarette smoke in my face just to try and get a rise out of me. I just ignored it. It doesn't bother me at all. The poor fellow just doesn't know what I know. I don't even mind if someone is drinking alcohol or half stoned. As long as they can follow my words and instructions, I'll keep talking. At some point, however, when dealing with an inebriated mind, you will need to leave. When I am invited to worldly birthday parties or weddings or something, and I feel to attend, I always make sure to arrive early to do my light-shining and then depart before anyone gets too drunk. That way, I can find the person who is open to the Lord and minister to them. Several times I have been able to effectively minister to a friend who was on the verge of being drunk, and a couple of them have actually been dramatically saved later on.

One time I had gone hunting with a group of my old friends from the world. For a few years after I came to the Lord, I made a real effort to be with them at least once or twice a year, just in case someone was open to God. They seemed to put up with me a little and with that strange feeling of conviction when I was around, though that subsided after they realized I was for real—that I wasn't going back to my old life and ways. And now I'm not invited to anything anymore (that's okay, I'm saved and in church!). They got used to my being with them on Saturday but departing early for church on Sunday. But on this occasion, I told them all ahead of time that I would be with them all weekend. However, the stipulation was that we were going to have a church service in the camp after the hunt, and I was going to preach. Though probably uncomfortable with that, they all agreed. At 10:30 the next morning, we're all sitting around the camp, and I realized *it's now or never.* So I nervously jumped up, laid my pickup tailgate down, got out my Bible, and announced that it was time. When I did that, every single one of the guys jumped up and ran to their comfort. Some ran to the beer cooler, some pulled out their tobacco chew or dip, and some lit up a cigarette. And then they all sat back down to listen to their friend-turned-preacher share the Word with them. They even asked me if it was okay to drink beer while I preached. Fine. I preached. No one was saved that day. But I did my part for world evangelism. Now ten years later, some of that group has since come to Christ and been filled with the Spirit. Some have attended our church. And some I've never seen again.

(By the way, follow my lead and never skip church for some secular pleasure, laziness, or people. It will taint your witness and your walk. When the world is coaching you with, "Come on, you don't have to go to church every week to be a Christian", do the exact opposite. The world and the devil *never* give right advice concerning God. We're either being conformed to the world, or we're transforming it. On the rare occasion that you must do a family thing that interrupts your church attendance, schedule your own evangelistic moment and share the gospel.)

The crux of the gospel is to major on the goodness of God—to present Him in the light of a merciful God and willing Father that loves people, and to help people receive that goodness in the form of miracles, blessing, and divine understanding. If you always come at it that way, you'll be able to look through the wickedness of people and touch them with a merciful message and tender spirit. So many times after a couple years of salvation, Christians develop a pious and cynical attitude toward sinners. Don't do that. Occasionally, if you detect that someone is resisting the grace of God, the right action is to explain the final judgment for a man without Christ—hell. And then maybe salvation will seem good.

23
It Takes Wisdom to Win Souls

...**and he that winneth souls is wise** (Proverbs 11:30).

Firstly, it is wise to win souls. When we arrive in heaven and stand before the Lord, it will be clear just how wise it was. Either we'll receive the promised *crown of rejoicing* (the soul-winner's crown) and treasure of a life lived right, or we won't. Our natural lives can be lived by fending for self and letting everyone else do the same, but our spiritual awakening demands that we help others awake. It is wise to acknowledge that now.

Secondly, it takes wisdom to lead others to Christ and to do it well. In the pulpit, the preacher must use wisdom to convey the challenge of the gospel in a real way. Just shouting and screaming with great, dramatic animations may wow a crowd, but the results will be fleeting. That's not wise. Out of the pulpit, the believer must use wisdom to lead others to Jesus. He cannot simply shout and quote and do all the talking. Rather, He must converse with precision. He cannot dump information on the sinner, but he must calculate his direction and time his words. He must ask questions, just like Jesus did, to lead the person in the direction of conviction and self assessment. The goal is to pry the person open and uncover the possible sticking points that have kept them from God. He must do his best to decipher the person's beliefs and give the right correction at the right time. He must allow the person to speak openly, ask questions, and ponder, rather than dump the truth on them all at once. At the same time, he must keep the person on track toward the next gospel point that needs to be made and not allow the person to drift away from the discussion with personal stories, difficulties, or wanderings. Finally, he must know when to strike with the challenge of salvation and commitment to Christ, and then repeat the process if necessary. To do it all well, he will need to follow the Holy Spirit.

When talking to a sinner, we must blend spiritual logic with simple proclamation. What I mean by that is that sometimes it is right to explain the scriptures and build the foundation for our spiritual truth, while other times (or at other points in the conversation), it is right to simply preach it, or tell it. That is the difference between teaching and preaching. Teachers explain it, while preachers tell it. Preachers spend more time telling what good things God has done for man. Teachers spend more time explaining man's responsibility to God. Though you may lean toward one or the other, witnessing requires the believer to do both. On one hand, it's possible to get tangled in questions and details while explaining and teaching. That's when we need to stop and just preach a short truth of the great salvation plan. On the other hand, it's also possible to get stuck just proclaiming the gospel that we don't notice the person has disconnected. That's when we need to stop, ask some questions, make the person tell what he thinks, and get him back on track with some teaching.

Here are some further wisdom tips, some from Charles Finney, one of the greatest revivalists in history.

1. If you have any feeling for a particular person, seize the opportunity quickly. Don't put off conversing with a sinner from day to day, thinking a better opportunity may come. Rather, make one. Go to him on purpose. Act as if promoting his salvation is a serious matter of business. In the person's eyes, they will notice that, at least to you, this is important.

2. Treat people kindly and respectfully. "But the wisdom that is from above is first pure, then peaceable, gentle, and easy to be entreated, full of mercy and good fruits, without partiality, and without hypocrisy. And the fruit of righteousness is sown in peace of them that make peace" (James 3:17-18). Notice the attributes of this wisdom that comes from God: pure, peaceable, gentle, full of mercy and good fruits. It appears that we can actually *see* wisdom at work. These attributes of wisdom are all exterior, meaning that they each have an outside effect on someone else. Basically, our compliance to these standards of wisdom will determine how effective our witness of Christ is toward people—how brightly or dimly our light will shine. We must show ourselves pure. We must be peaceable and gentle with folks, and we should show great mercy toward people without hypocrisy or partiality. We'd better get all racism, cynicism, and lukewarm-ism out of us, or it will come out of us in front of someone. You are not seeking a quarrel with anyone. And it's your burden not to let it become one.

3. Be solemn and be plain. Avoid all lightness and levity. Recall the demeanor of a pastor giving a salvation altar call—he is serious and not silly or jovial. That is the right demeanor for such a serious matter. And don't cover up any circumstance of the person's character. The goal is to address his conscience and point him to the guilt in his own heart and mind. That is the target for this salvation plan you are presenting. Make the person realize that you are talking about *him*. Address *his* life, *his* issues, and *his* unbelief so that you awaken his conscience. There is no need to glide over the thing that might make a sinner uncomfortable. Rather, the more of his "rocks" that are kicked over, the deeper his salvation will be.
4. Be attentive to the effect of the conversation, and then get to the point. When you notice someone is opening, press in that direction and bring them to a decision shortly.

Again, though, so you don't get bogged down with rules, let me keep this balanced with an exception story. I once knew a Methodist woman who testified of her salvation this way: she was working as a bank drive-through teller, when a young man came through. During the transaction, he asked through the microphone if she knew where she would go when she died, heaven or hell? She answered, "Well, I'm Catholic, so I guess I'll go to heaven." The young man responded sharply through the microphone, "Lady, if that's all you got, then you're going to hell! You need Jesus Christ!" And then he drove off. Now to some degree, as you can tell, this goes against some of our rules and principles. But when it gets results, and when it's led by the Spirit, I'm all for it. The woman said that she went home completely distraught, scared, and under conviction.

That night, she got on her knees and asked Jesus Christ into her life, and was saved.

> **"It is a matter of fact, a historical truth, that he that winneth souls is wise. Success in saving souls is evidence that a man understands the gospel, and understands human nature, that he knows how to adapt means to his end; that he has common sense, and that kind of tact, that practical discernment, to know how to get at people."**
>
> —Charles Finney

Colossians 4:5,6 reads, "Walk in wisdom toward them that are without, redeeming the time. Let your speech be alway with grace, seasoned with salt, that ye may know how ye ought to answer every man." Moffat's translation reads, "Let Christian wisdom rule your behavior to the outside world."

Witness Principle 27

Whatever It Takes, Get Wisdom

And finally, James Chapter 1 instructs you to ask God for wisdom, and He will give it. The stipulation is that you must desperately want it, and you must fully believe that He will give it. And then you must accept it by faith. Pray like Paul did in Ephesians 1:17-18, that "…God…may give to you the spirit of wisdom and revelation…" And pray it until something in you changes. Whatever it takes, get more wisdom.

24
Believe in the Power of the Word

In these next few chapters, I will detail some effective, powerful means of sharing the message of Jesus Christ. And I will do it in order of complexity, or of amount of scriptural knowledge required.

This first means of gospel presentation is the easiest and quickest way to spread the gospel, and it only requires the believer to know one gospel truth. Just one. It is this: believe that there is power in God's written Word, and give it to people. Don't give Bibles. Give a short gospel presentation. Give Bibles to Christians, but give the short gospel of salvation to sinners—on paper, on cell phones, on computers—however you can. Use gospel tracts, use text messages, use emails, use videos and phone apps, use DVDs—whatever you've got. And never, never, never, underestimate the power of God's written Word.

You don't need to even memorize what's in the gospel tract nor what you copy/paste from a good gospel website. You only need to give it. Ignore those who say that handing gospel pamphlets is weird or ineffective. Again, believe in the power of God's Word. God did. God believes in the written Word. He started it all when He wrote words on stone tablets with His finger. Then He had Moses write words for the Book of the Law and prophets to write more. Then He had apostles write letters to churches. Then He urged Christians to compile the words into a Bible. Now He inspires preachers to write books. And He also encourages believers to print tracts and hand them out. If the Apostle Paul were here today, don't you think he would have a digital printing operation, a computer, a media production department, a web site, and a Facebook page? Certainly he would. So do we. And so does every other minister or believer who believes in the Word of God. Didn't the Word of God change your life? Just remember that it can do the same for anyone.

> **WITNESS PRINCIPLE 28**
>
> Never Underestimate the Power of God's Written Word

T.L. Osborn began his soul-winning lifestyle at age twelve. He purchased a toy printing press and printed gospel tracts on scraps of paper for his town of 350 people. But he didn't stop there, at one point, his ministry was printing over one ton of literature a day and even dropping millions of leaflets from airplanes into heathen countries.

Angelo Mitropoulos came to America from Greece in the 1970's. About eight months after a Christian led him to the Lord, he was driving an ice cream truck in upstate New York. The Lord got his attention by pointing out all the thousands of customers he was seeing every summer, and Angelo accepted the call of the Christian. He knew the Spirit wanted him to share Christ with everyone who bought an ice cream from him. The problem was, he couldn't speak, read, or write English. So, Angelo went to a Christian bookstore and saw some gospel bookmarks that contained some scriptures on them. He knew he needed thousands of copies, but he didn't plan to buy them. Rather, he designed, cut, and taped up his own bookmark, added the plan of salvation and a prayer to be saved, and went to a copy store to make black and white copies to give away. Within three months, he had distributed over 10,000 gospel tracts to his ice cream customers. That, too, became quite expensive, so he eventually bought an offset printing press to print the gospel in mass quantities. During his ministry, he printed millions of gospel tracts and effectively distributed them through the hands of church members, convincing them that all they had to do was saturate their city with the Word of God. And if they did, God could save sinners. He went on to own scores of printing presses and to sell and give many away for others to multiply the Word of God. I was one. Angelo called me one day and said, "In prayer last night, the Lord told me to give you a printing press." I drove up to Tulsa, picked up a whole print shop, spent two days in training on the equipment, and brought it back to my garage to spread the gospel. Before I switched to farming out my printing projects professionally, that one little AB Dick 360 offset press printed over 1 million gospel tracts. Angelo certainly believed in the power of God's Word. And so do I.

Handing a little piece of paper to someone seems insignificant and boring. It seems foolish. And with all the possible nuts and flakes on the streets handing out leaflets, it seems embarrassing. But it is sometimes the best way to get the message of Christ to a sinner. The tract can go home with them. The tract can stay in their house for months or even years. The tract can preach in your place. The tract will not intimidate them nor prompt them to argue. The tract doesn't get discouraged. The written Word knows no fear and flinches in the face of no man. And the tract never forgets its message. I have one friend who told me that the moment he received Christ, he had an instant flashback to the first seed that was planted in him. Two years prior, he remembered that while "hanging out" in his sister's bathroom, he had read a certain gospel 'Chick' cartoon tract. He didn't respond to it at the time, but immediately when the light of salvation hit his soul, he realized how it must have impacted him deep down. God's Word has power, and seeds can last forever.

Here is what you can do with gospel literature, CDs, DVDs, and all media.

1. Hand gospel literature to strangers throughout your day: cashiers, waiters, hostesses, bank tellers, people in the malls, people everywhere. When you hand it out, you can say something like, "God bless you." Or, "Have a nice day." Or, "This is a message from the Bible." Or, "Are you saved? Here this will help you." Or, if saying something is still too scary for you, just shove it into their hand and run off as fast as you can.

2. Hide gospel literature everywhere. When you go to the store, you can work covertly and never speak to anyone. Simply take a pack of gospel tracts to the grocery store with you and go to the book / magazine section. Slip one tract in each romance novel, and be on your way. Head over to the beer aisle (or soda aisle) and shove a gospel tract in each beer box. Don't look around and be suspicious. Just work quickly. And then get off the aisle fast so no one who knows you sees you and stumbles, thinking you're a beer drinker. If you get caught by the workers and told to stop, just comply, hand them a tract to

keep for themselves, and stop your covert work for that store. You can do the same in clothes stores—hide them in pants pockets or jacket pockets or purses. Whatever you do, don't litter the store, but ensure that the tracts are hidden until customers get home. Then the tract can pop out and introduce Jesus.

3. Leave gospel pamphlets behind in restaurant restrooms, post offices, gas pumps—anywhere. Don't make a mess, but leave the 'bread of life' as you go about your day.
4. Post the gospel to Facebook, Twitter, and text messages. Share gospel phone apps that have good Bible teaching and preaching content.
5. For several years, our church designed and ordered custom acrylic retail displays that would hold about 40 CDs. Church members would approach convenience store / restaurant managers and request that we leave our glamorous box of CDs near the cashier for people to take for free. This way, rather than just hand things to people who didn't want them, those who were interested could get a gospel message for free. The church members would frequent the store and refill the box when it was empty, and within a couple years, we had distributed over 5,000 CDs. Our church grew because of it, and our people found a way to make a difference in someone's life. Since then, we have provided church members with free CDs and DVDs to hand out just like literature. Again, if we believe the Word of God is life-changing, why not give it to someone else?

One day after church my wife and I and several of us were eating in a restaurant. We handed a gospel tract to the waiter, saying something like, "We know you didn't get to go to church today, so here is a message for you from God." He stopped what he was doing, knelt down near the table, and began reading it. After about a minute, he looked up with anticipation, and I asked him if he believed what he had read and if he wanted to be saved. He said, "Yes", and he wanted to do it right then. Right next to our table, kneeling low, Rueben asked Jesus into his life and was saved. After he had prayed, I asked why he so quickly believed as he read the tract. He pointed to a line in the tract and said, "Right there. It says that *...a saved person is no longer lost.* And I've been feeling very lost in my life." Praise the Lord. We ended up teaching Rueben at his home a few times and even baptized him in his bathtub, helping him along his journey.

Another time early in my ministry I had gone to the local high school to speak to the 'Students for Christ' group. I decided to put the kids to work and help them reach their school for Jesus. So I brought them 4500 tracts to get into the hands of every high school student, and had this little group of 20 Christian teenagers saturate the school—every friend, every teacher, every classmate, and every locker. (You know, it's legal for kids to talk about Jesus at school or even hand out a piece of paper. That's a first amendment right of the Constitution, as long as they don't disrupt class or break a school rule while doing it.) Well, that was exciting for the kids, but summer had come, and I never got a chance to see the group again and get a status report. That summer, I was walking a neighborhood with our outreach team and came across two certain people. One was a teacher from that school, who saw the tracts we were handing out and excitedly claimed, "I was given one of these at school. I'm a Christian. God bless you!" The other was a teenage boy in the neighborhood, who said the same thing, except he wasn't saved. He said he had received one of the same pamphlets at school and had read it. I asked if he prayed the prayer at the end, but he had not. I said, "Would you like to now?" He did, we did, and he was saved. Glory to God! Never underestimate the power of God's Word.

25
Presenting the Gospel

How many times have you wanted to share Christ with someone, but you just couldn't maneuver the conversation where you wanted it? Rather than force an awkward moment, you let the opportunity pass. Part of the issue is your confidence, or lack thereof, in the details of what to say. But I waited this long in the book to share the technical preaching aspect of witnessing to avoid overwhelming you with memorization. Really, when we lean on honesty and heartfelt sincerity, the Spirit of God will empower us and smooth the uncomfortable moments. Rather than get bogged down in formal strategy, what you share with people needs to come from your heart rather than your head. If you don't have much in your heart, don't say much. Just whatever you do say, say it with faith and love. God does the rest.

These next methods of gospel presentation involve you speaking more—explaining and preaching the simple gospel in an effective manner. The goal is to turn the conversation in the direction you want it, beginning with any bait or any nicety that you can think of or hear from God, and getting the person in a place to hear the salvation message. And these are not the only methods. They just seem to be fairly effective. If you'll get started and look to the Lord, He may put together a perfect, unique approach just for you. Or as you commit to this great call, you may tap into the power of God with words of knowledge, prophecy, or other gifts of the Spirit for people as you get into a conversation. Whatever you do, be yourself. And know that God is with you.

Method 1—Are You Saved?

Whether stranger, acquaintance, friend or family, we don't usually know if they have yet believed on the Lord Jesus Christ. We don't know if they are saved or not. So, why not ask them? In a pure, heartfelt manner, we can always ask, "Are you saved?" Or, "Are you born again?" That gets right to the point, doesn't it? Some will say that we shouldn't use Bible terminology or spiritual terms when we witness. But I disagree. Spiritual terms are valid and essential. When using the term 'saved' or 'salvation' or 'born again', you can quickly recognize where the person is. Immediately, you'll discern if the person has any clue of salvation through Jesus Christ, and you can take it from there. If the person answers, "Yes", then you can affirm their salvation with some excitement and maybe a follow up question of, "Oh, great. When did you accept Jesus as your Savior?" Or, you may state, "Oh, praise the Lord, so you are born again already? That is wonderful!" Or you may ask them, "How do you know you are saved?" And again, notice how the person reacts. We want to

> **WITNESS PRINCIPLE 29**
>
> Method 1—
>
> Are You Saved?

give people more light if they need it, or rejoice with them if they already have it.

After asking "Are you saved?", you can do the *gospel two step*:

> **Step 1: Believe.** See if they believe the message of Jesus that you share with them.
> **Step 2: Receive.** If they believe it, have them receive Jesus by praying with you.

This makes it so easy. We don't need to pressure ourselves to win an argument or persuade some hard heart. Rather, we are just looking for someone who believes. Regardless of *how* you preach Jesus Christ to them, you are only watching to *see if* they believe you. If they do, it is easy—just help them confess it. If they don't, you are done. Just move on.

Scripture gives us this simple two-step,

> **...if you confess with your mouth Jesus as Lord, and believe in your heart that God raised Jesus from the dead, you shall be saved; for with the heart man believes, resulting in righteousness, and with the mouth he confesses, resulting in salvation** (Romans 10:9-10).

Is it that easy? Certainly. God designed it that way. Now, we don't always know how deeply someone believed, so the ground of their heart will determine their future, and only God knows the future. But we can do our part to get them through the Door. Angelo testifies of his salvation this way: he said that while working at his pizza shop, a man came to his town on a several week business trip. He said several times the man came to eat pizza, and each time he tried to persuade Angelo to receive Christ. Angelo would watch him at his table, as the man would ruin his oven-hot pizza by praying over it for five minutes and letting it get cold. But the man wouldn't stop talking to him about Jesus. Finally, out of desperation just to get the man to leave him alone, Angelo reluctantly agreed to repeat a prayer with the man. They prayed, and the man left. Angelo thought it was all over. But then realized something had changed within him. He had a desire for God. A day or two later, a group of local Christians came over (whom the man had pointed to Angelo) and invited Angelo to a home Bible study. Angelo couldn't wait to go. His reluctant confession of Christ had saved his soul. And the rest is history.

My wife's friend, Dawn, was saved in a similar fashion. She testifies that a neighbor friend of hers had started coming over to talk about Jesus. And though Dawn was very uncomfortable with it and had no desire for spiritual things, she didn't want to hurt the neighbor's feelings. So she let it continue a few times. Finally, Dawn decided that she would just go ahead and say "the prayer" to get this over with so they could go back to just being friends. And voila, she "accidentally" got saved and later became a preacher.

This strategy works really well with Catholics as well. Many Catholics already believe in God and Jesus and even in the resurrection of Jesus. They just sometimes have no idea how to be saved. I like to explain to them how they've taken the first step toward God by believing, but that they might have missed the second step (For even the devil believes in God, Jesus, and the resurrection, but he's certainly not saved). The second step is to confess with their mouth and submit to Jesus as their Lord. That involves a confession of commitment. They need to know that this is important and that it is the catalyst for salvation. After they pray, I encourage them to begin to learn the Bible and find out what God wants of them. The Catholic needs some good Bible teaching after they've committed to Christ, so point them to a Bible teaching source, or give them some CDs, books, web site videos, etc. Or take them to church with you. If they are concerned about remaining Catholic, inform them that they can keep being Catholic as long as they promise to learn, believe, and obey the New Testament. They can even use their Catholic Bible *New Testament* (it's the exact same as any King James Version, but we want to remove all the little mental obstacles for them until God gets hold of them).

Our one, self-published tract is that exact message, "Are You Saved?" It gets right to the point—just the way I like it. And it's helped thousands of people receive the Lord.

Method 2—The Roman Road

You can use The Roman Road to lead someone to Christ. Using a few precise scriptures from this one book of the Bible, you can let the Bible present the gospel for you. Use the scriptures to explain these key points to the sinner.

1. **Romans 3:23** – Admit that you are a sinner. "For all have sinned and fall short of the glory of God." We all have sin in our hearts. We all were born with sin. We were born under the power of sin's control. If the person has a hard time realizing that we are born with sin, use the term 'our selfish and greedy nature.' And explain that because of Adam and Eve choosing to sin in the beginning, they chose death (spiritual death), or sin nature, for everyone. Even babies, as innocent as they are, display the selfish, greedy nature of sin, as they make demands and have no care for others' well being, throwing tantrums or fits of frustration at will. They have no spiritual connection with God until they believe and are 'born again'.

2. **Romans 6:23a** – Understand that you deserve death for your sin. "...the wages of sin is death..." Sin has an ending. It begins with spiritual death (separation from God) and ends with *eternal* spiritual death (eternal separation from God). Physical death is a result of the 'original' sin, and funerals are a sad, traumatic time for people. But even worse is *eternal, spiritual* death. The Bible explains that there is a place called the Lake of Fire which is a place of eternal torment that was prepared for the devil, demons, and death itself. But because of sin, humans who remain lost and unsaved will also be cast into the Lake of Fire to be tormented forever (Revelation 20:15). In no way is God pleased to see people neglect His salvation plan, but the spiritual justice system is already set. Picture it this way, *Satan shows up to the sinner's doorstep, knocks, and when the door opens, he says, "Hello, you have remained in sin and done very well at your life without God, and now I would like to pay you for your efforts, here is eternal death."*

3. **Romans 6:23b** – But God had a plan to save us. "...But the gift of God is eternal life through Jesus Christ our Lord." Before the world began, God knew mankind would choose sin and death. But because He could not violate man's free will and force His holiness upon us, He designed a backup plan! God decided that He would come to earth Himself in the form of His Son, Jesus Christ, and pay for our sins with His own blood. He did it. God has given us our salvation as a gift. You can't earn this gift, but you must reach out and accept it by faith.

Romans 5:8 – "God demonstrates His own love for us, in that while we were yet sinners Christ died for us." God loved us, even while we were separated from Him. And He allowed His holy Son to shed His sinless blood as the replacement for the death wages we all deserved.

4. **Romans 10:13** – If you want to be saved, call out to God. "Whoever will call on the name of the Lord will be saved." If you believe the truth you have heard, now it is time to accept this salvation. Receive Jesus Christ as your Lord by inviting Him into your heart and life. The miracle of salvation happens when you believe, and when you say something with your mouth.

   Romans 10:9,10 – "...If you confess with your mouth Jesus as Lord, and believe in your heart that God raised Jesus from the dead, you shall be saved; for with the heart man believes, resulting in righteousness, and with the mouth he confesses, resulting in salvation."

Keep your key witnessing goal in mind: you are only looking to see if they believe. If they believe, lead them in a confession of faith—something like,

> ***"God, save me. I believe in Jesus Christ— that He is the Son of God and that He died for my sins. I believe He rose from the dead. Forgive me. Clean me and make me new in Christ. Jesus, give me eternal life, be my Lord, and come live in my heart. I commit my life to You forever. Thank you, Lord. Now I'm saved."***

If the person prays to receive Jesus, tell them that they are now a child of God, forgiven and accepted by God. Minister to them in any other way the Spirit leads you, and help them get to a good church if you can. On a side note, some people teach that we should never ask if a new believer felt anything after praying to receive Christ. But I think sometimes it's okay. Occasionally, people don't sense anything at all, but most of the time, they do. I like to use it as an opportunity to reinforce the truth of what 'born again' means. Jesus compared the born again experience to the wind—that it's hard to explain, but you know it's there. And then sometimes, people are really touched with feelings of warmth, love, peace, joy, hope, or some flutter in their heart. Many times after people pray to receive Christ, they just can't stop smiling. They know something has happened, and it just feels good. I like to share in that with them and be excited with them. If, perhaps, they didn't sense anything, then I explain that it's not about a feeling, and that over time, they'll recognize some changes in their heart because what they did was real and of the Lord.

WITNESS PRINCIPLE 30

Method 2—The Roman Road

You may explain that their name is now written in heaven, and there is an inheritance awaiting them there. But also explain that they have already received the first part of that inheritance—the Holy Spirit. When a person receives Christ, they get something (some*one*) *immediately!*

Method 3—Your ABCs

Here is another easy gospel presentation to use—remember your ABCs. Find what you feel comfortable with, and it can become your standard approach. As you develop and grow in the Lord, you will be open to further leading of the Spirit and possibly a greater arsenal of knowledge or methods, but these basic gospel presentations work perfectly for most cases of getting people through the Door. Here are the ABCs of salvation:

> **A**cknowledge that they are a sinner.
> **B**elieve in Jesus Christ.
> **C**onfess Jesus Christ as Savior and Lord.

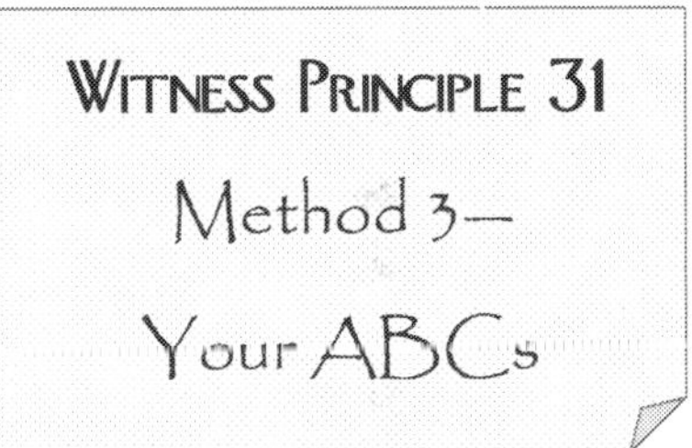

A. **Acknowledge that they are a sinner.**
In order to be saved, the first thing is to acknowledge that they are a sinner. "For all have sinned and come short of the glory of God" (Romans 3:23).

B. **Believe In Jesus Christ.**
"Believe on the Lord Jesus Christ and you will be saved..." (Acts 16:31).

"As many as received Him, to them He gave the right to become children of God, to those who believe in His name" (John 1:12).

"For God so loved the world that He gave His only begotten Son, that whosoever believes in Him should not perish, but have everlasting life" (John 3:16).

C. **Confess Jesus Christ as Savior and Lord.**
"Whoever confesses that Jesus is the Son of God, God abides in him and he in God" (1 John 4:15).

"...If you confess with your mouth Jesus as Lord, and believe in your heart that God raised Jesus from the dead, you shall be saved" (Romans 10:9).

Again, your witnessing goal? You are only looking to see if they believe. If they believe, lead them in a confession of faith—something like,

> "*God, save me. I believe in Jesus Christ—that He is the Son of God and that He died for my sins. I believe He rose from the dead. Forgive me. Clean me and make me new in Christ. Jesus, give me eternal life, be my Lord, and come live in my heart. I commit my life to You forever. Thank you, Lord. Now I'm saved.*"

26
How to Talk to Jehovah Witnesses, Muslims, Mormons, Jews, and Atheists

I realize this is one of the major pressure points of witnessing—that at some point, we might find ourselves in a conversation with one of these false religion pushers, and we don't know exactly how to handle them. Well, I admit, a conversation with any of them will be convoluted and confusing. Why? Because all false religions and doctrines are *confused.* They are doctrines of demons. Make no mistake about it. They are all devil-driven, dark, and destructive. And they keep many honest people headed to hell. But after much experience with most of them, I can help you. I've studied many of their messages, methods, and their conversion strategies, and I will share a few things to greatly assist you. But it's not necessary to get too detailed in dissecting their convoluted beliefs. It's better to just stick to our *right* message.

No matter what, remember that you have the higher spiritual authority in every encounter. You are backed up by God, and they are not. You have a responsibility to run the show *your* way or *no* way. So, never let them yank you around onto their tricky road. Never let them manipulate you down some difficult path of questions. Rather, do what Jesus did. He ran the show. If He didn't want to answer a question from the Pharisees, He didn't. He would simply ask *them* a question—He redirected it to where He wanted the conversation to go.

Remember, only *spend time* with the honest, open hearted ones. This eliminates many of our false religion encounters. If ever a person is coming at you to persuade you toward their religion, rarely will you be able to persuade them of *yours.* There are a few good things you can say to leave them with some shocking seeds of truth. But for the most part, they are hard ground and usually end up wasting your time.

I was in Chicago with Angelo on my first downtown street adventure, and we were working with our teams passing out flyers and leading people to Jesus. I got into a conversation with a young Muslim man, and we began our back and forth Christ vs. Muhammad, God vs. Allah arguments. I was doing fairly well it seemed, but the young Muslim was holding his own. Of course he was wrong. But that's the frustrating part, isn't it, when one person is right and the other *thinks* they're right? After about 15 minutes, I remember Angelo walking by me and motioning me to come ahead and leave the man. But I sort of waived him off, thinking that I might really be getting somewhere with the guy. After another 15 or 20 minutes, I finally gave up and went to find my team. Angelo approached me and asked how it went. I gave my blah, blah, blah. And he corrected me. He said, "Chas, while you spent 30 to 40 minutes arguing with that false religion guy, you missed hundreds of others walking by you." The point: no matter how right we are (and we're very right, of course) we must be wise in choosing who to spend time on.

Overall, the best thing you can do is just tell them the truth—that Jesus died for their sins and that He is the only *way*. If it's hard to get a good word in, just stop the person, and say something like this, "Please hold on for a second and let me just say what I need to say. Then we can part. Jesus Christ is the only way..." And speak enough to get the good news to them. Then leave without waiting for a response.

Jehovah Witnesses

They have been lied to. They don't believe Jesus Christ is the only begotten Son of God, nor that His sacrifice is the only way to salvation. They are told not to ever let Christians pray for them or lead them in prayer. They are told to never accept any literature from Christians. They have a Bible, but it has been altered with scriptures both changed and omitted, mostly by trying to erase the deity of Christ. They will begin by asking you some leading questions to detect if you have any fears of world events, or blah, blah, blah...it really doesn't matter. And they always have about five pet doctrines they have been taught—all found in Scripture somewhere, but all twisted into lies. This is why you should know your Bible, at least some key scriptures and a general framework of understanding. If you don't know much, just follow your previous instructions: don't tell them much. Just be joyful and loving, let them know how Jesus saved your soul, and point them on their way.

Here is what you can do when they come to your door. First, they usually come in pairs. One person is the veteran, and the other person is the rookie who is learning. Ignore the veteran, but preach to the rookie. Even if the veteran is doing all the talking and you are conversing with them, even if your eye contact is with the veteran, you're actually planting good seed in the rookie. That young one isn't fully indoctrinated, so there may be a better chance to alter their course. Though the veteran will try to protect the rookie, your seed will go a long way. Next, before they leave, tell them that if they ever want to be saved, to "Just say, God, save me. I believe Jesus Christ is the Son of God." And, "Come see me if you ever need help or if you are ever sick. Jesus Christ will heal you." Lastly, if you ever see their literature lying around at the post office, or stuck in a neighbor's door handle, remove it, throw it away, and replace it with your own gospel tract! That may sound quite gutsy, but don't we have, not only a right, but an obligation to protect the innocent from the twisted? Yes, we do.

I do not wish to convolute this chapter by including detailed Jehovah Witness beliefs and arguments, so for specific scriptures and to disprove their false doctrine, refer to our web site page (www.StevensonMinistries.org/jehovah_witnesses).

Muslims (Islam)

They, too, have been lied to. Their religion has told them that Jesus lived. He did. They believe that Jesus was a prophet (along with Muhammad and a few others). Jesus was. They believe Jesus ministered on the earth. They believe Jesus worked miracles. They believe Jesus ascended to heaven and is alive (they will even admit that Muhammad is dead and Jesus is in heaven). They even believe Jesus will come back one day to the earth. All true. *But*...they have been taught that Jesus *never died.* They say God took him alive from off the mountain up to heaven and that the Jews fabricated the whole story of the cross, the death, and the resurrection. The devil has tricked them into taking out the most essential piece of the puzzle. If Jesus never died, then there is no payment for sin. If He never rose from the dead, then we are yet in our sins and there is no salvation. What a deception!

And that is how I minister to them. Almost every time I get into a conversation with a Muslim, I maneuver the conversation around to what they believe about Jesus. Then I sternly warn them, "Listen to what I'm about to tell you. You are deceived. The devil has deceived you, your family, and your whole religion into taking out the one piece of Christianity that is most essential. You accept some of the facts of Jesus Christ, but leave out the pivotal, spiritual, life-altering event of His blood sacrifice. You will never have peace and love in your heart until you change your belief. And you will end up in hell if you don't."

The Islamic religion is a very harsh religion. They believe "Allah" is the creator, and they live to please him (so they think). But they do not believe in him as a father. God as our Father is an essential identification for Christians that denotes a parental love, mercy, tenderness, forgiveness, and protection from evil. The Muslims do not have that. They are *not* taught that God can be their heavenly Father. So they live with a dread and a fear of "Allah", knowing they never please him enough. I always remind them of that—that if they will receive Jesus, the Son of God, God will adopt them into His family, forgive them of sin, and be a loving Father to them. Some have accepted what I've said and received Jesus. But most have not. Now, I look to speak less and shoot my arrows with precision. So should you. Oh yes, one final thing. The Muslims have been taught that our Christian Bible has been wrongly translated and skewed, and they will sometimes harp on that a while. If that is where the conversation is bogged down, then it's time to get out anyway.

Mormons

They've been distracted. And it is such a shame because they are so close to being true believers in Christ. Actually, I've met Mormons who really might be saved, even though they hardly know it. If you talk to one, you will find that they believe many of the same things we do. I mean, they're taught the Bible fairly well, and they're usually really good people. But there is a problem. They don't preach that Jesus Christ is the only way to eternal life and forgiveness of sins. They deny that Jesus is one with God. And they don't believe in the person of the Holy Spirit (they think He is just a mist or an electricity of God or something). The worst thing is that the further one goes in Mormonism, the more sinister their practices become, with secret temple rituals and strange marriage and ordination commands, thus making it an occult.

The other odd thing is this "book of Mormon" that they propagate. It seems strange that they want to peddle this *dead* book, when 99% of their real lifestyle is from the Bible. But really, we know why: first, it is because the devil has deceived and distracted them. And second, it is because touting a special new thing like "a missing testament" is a human means of gaining importance and prominence. For years, I would ask every Mormon to please tell me something of the book of Mormon that I need to know. "Just tell me one important scripture or truth that isn't already in the Bible. I mean, if there's something good in it, I want to know." But no one ever could. They always just said, "Well, you need to read it." What a joke. Finally, one day a Mormon admitted to me what was in it. He said that the book of Mormon (given by the "angel" Moroni and "found" by Joseph Smith) was the missing account of Jesus' ministry during the 40 days He walked the earth after His resurrection—that He came over to the Americas and preached to the native Indians! But, still, no one is ever able to give me any essential truth that it contains. They can't, because it's not of God. And I certainly don't study any false teaching to find out for myself. So, all we can do is love them and lead them out of darkness if they are willing. To do anything further, following the Spirit in what to say or how to act is our only chance.

Unbelieving Jews

Unbelieving Jews have been deceived. They are still waiting for their Savior to come. But He has already come. (Obviously, many Jews believe in Jesus, so they are Christians. This chapter is dealing with ones who don't believe, but who practice Judaism.) Most unbelieving Jews that you will encounter will not be extreme orthodox Jews, but rather nominal ones who identify with Judaism only by race and only practice Judaism on their main religious days. As a matter of fact, you will probably know their Torah better than they do. You will know their Old Covenant better than they ever did. And because of that, you may be able to get somewhere with them. I remember sitting in a Jewish jeweler's office one day. He had an Old Testament on his desk, but he had no idea why he believed what he believed. I quoted a couple of scriptures from Psalms that he was startled to hear. He even opened his book and found them. I always deal with the sin issue when talking with unbelieving Jews. The Old Law required blood sacrifice in order for God to overlook sins. But none of them sacrifice animals today. I always tell them that "*without the shedding of blood, there is no remission of sins.*" And that that is why they have no closeness to God. Of course, their answer for stopping the animal sacrifices comes from their new "Rabbinical law", which they say supersedes the law of Moses. The rabbis decided that when the temple was destroyed in 70 AD, then God no longer required the blood, and all they need to do is pray toward the temple and ask for forgiveness like Solomon requested. Nonsense—another human guess at a heavenly truth. I'm not saying that animal sacrifices are still applicable—they most certainly are not. I'm saying that the blood of Jesus satisfied the 'life for a life' principle of God pardoning sin. Isaiah 53 and Psalm 22 are good Old Testament chapters that you could lead the Jewish person through if they will let you. These chapters are the prophecies of what the true ending and purpose of the Messiah would be—His death on the cross and the significance of His blood sacrifice—exactly what the New Testament reveals and what history confirms.

Atheists

They are all liars. For atheists to say they don't believe in a Creator is a lie. The Bible says,

> **For the invisible things of Him from the creation of the world are clearly seen, being understood by the things that are made, even his eternal power and Godhead; so that they are without excuse...they became fools...** (Romans 1:20-22).

I was recently talking with one of our great soul-winners at church, Emilio. He said to me, "You know, atheists are the dumbest people in the whole world. And next time I meet one, I am going to tell him personally, You are the dumbest person in the whole world." That made me laugh. What a great ministry to an atheist. Why are they dumb? Because when we look around at this earth, it is clear that Someone made it. And there is no excuse for them lying to their own conscience. A prominent university once conducted an interesting study. They tested approximately 440 admitted atheists on a lie-detector machine. The key question they asked each one was, "Do you believe in God. They all said, "No." But the machine said otherwise. The machine verified that they were all lying. Deep down, everyone knows there is a God. Even evolutionists, who are blinded by very flimsy scientific theories, know there is a God. The problem is that their pride causes them to hide from Him so they can continue being their own god, leading their own self-indulgent lives—before journeying to hell. "The fool has said in his heart, There is no God" (Psalm 14:1).

What else can you tell an atheist if you don't want to be so blunt? "Okay, I hear what you are saying, but one day when you own up to the fact that God is real and that you are not accepted by Him, believe in Jesus Christ and ask Him to save you. He will. Bye bye."

27
Baptize Them

I want to mention this because of the spiritual significance and tangible excitement that can happen at water baptism and also because of the false perception of water baptism—that it's some restricted religious right reserved only for the pastors and priests. It is not. Water baptism is a command, but the means and order of it is not. The word 'baptism' is not a sacred theological word. It really is only a Greek word that should have been translated into English like all the other words. It simply means 'to dunk' or 'to submerge' or 'to cover with completely'. And any believer can do it to another.

Jesus commanded it. The apostles did it. Philip the deacon servant did it. And I believe we should do it. I've just always been a Bible guy—a Word person, so if it's in the Word, particularly the New Testament, it's for me. The only exception might be the "give the brethren a holy kiss" scripture. I think I'll stick to the holy hug and a handshake, thank you very much. But in accepting the call of the Christian, leading others to Jesus, I know of no reason not to dunk people in water after they receive Jesus as Lord. What I discovered was something very powerful—something even spiritually tangible. The New Testament is void of most all ceremonial ordinances, since all outward law and carnal commands are not necessary after the blood of Jesus. The only two outward, ceremonial commands that remain for us are baptism in water and communion.

Baptism in water is *not* required for a person to be saved, but it is the first command given to a saved person. I realize that Jesus said in Mark 16:16 "He who believes and is baptized will be saved; but he who does not believe will be condemned." And if we only had that one scripture, at first glance it appears that the act of water baptism in water is necessary for salvation. But our primary rule of Bible interpretation is that any one scripture must be interpreted in light of other scriptures. And we have many other scriptures that don't mention baptism in water as an absolute for the saving of the soul. For instance, Romans 10:9-10 says to "believe and confess." John 3:16 says to "believe", etc. And neither of those even mention water baptism. Furthermore, if we examine what Jesus said, notice that He didn't say "…he who is not water baptized will be condemned", but only "…he who *doesn't believe* will be condemned."

Witness Principle 33

You Can Baptize People in Water

So baptism in water doesn't save a person, but it is the correct action of a saved person. Jesus commanded it for a reason. Something spiritually significant takes place when a person is dunked, and it takes place in their own soul—in their own mind. At salvation, a person is sealed in their heart by the Holy Spirit. But at water baptism, the physical act seals something in their minds. It is a moment of clarity and commitment. And it is a proclamation to the world and the Church that *my life is not my own, I am dedicated to another.* It is an outward evidence of an inward heart change. And I say that it is somewhat like a "permission slip" to follow Jesus. For example, a kid could sneak onto the school bus for the field trip without a slip. And that kid could arrive at the same destination as everyone else. But they wanted him to turn in a signed permission slip like they said.

I had a friend in the ministry who always chuckled at my determination to get new believers baptized. He even called me a Bapticostal (you get it: Baptist beliefs combined with Pentecostal beliefs). But it was all in fun, since we both knew and believed the Word of God—that baptism was real and right. So, I just keep baptizing people. I baptize them as soon as they are willing, and I do it in whatever water is available. I've dunked people in public water fountains, swimming pools, theme parks, Jacuzzis, bathtubs, rivers, and oceans. And it doesn't matter to me if we're both wearing nice dress clothes. I used to take church teams out to apartments and communities, preach on a loud speaker, and baptize all the new converts in a portable plastic kiddy pool that we carried with us to fill up on-site.

One time I was in Harlem, New York, preaching in a drug rehab home, and several people accepted Christ. One of them really wanted to serve and obey God, so he asked what he should do next. I informed the group that it was time to get dunked in water and then asked the leaders if there was any water around. "There is a river down behind the ghetto, but it's really muddy and dirty," was their response. But that was good enough for me. About 20 of us trekked through the neighborhood about a quarter mile to the river, and I walked out into it. But "muddy" wasn't the right word! It was soft bottom mud, and I sunk in up to my knees. Each step into the water was a treacherous slide into two feet of mud, rocks, and debris. I walked out as deep as I could, and informed the men to carry the ladies out if they still wanted to obey Jesus under these circumstances. They all adamantly determined to do it. And so we did. In the muddy goop, they were all baptized in the name of the Lord Jesus Christ. I would never turn down someone's enthusiastic devotion to God.

I had one friend who came to me ready to commit his life to the Lord. He wanted to be baptized immediately, that night. This was before I was pastor of a church with a building key and authority to fill the baptismal, so I took him to the fountain outside the church. The only problem was that it was in January, and it was 35 degrees outside! But he didn't care, so I didn't care. We jumped in the two foot deep, ice water pond, sat down, and under he went! I believe that to obey God is more important than circumstantial luxury or convenience. Even when we schedule baptism in our church, I always open it up to anyone in the service at that moment. I know they didn't bring a change of clothes. But that's okay. They can ride home wet. The early saints didn't have changing rooms down at the river. They had to walk home dripping wet through the dusty streets, with mud caking on their feet, right in front of all the mockers and scoffers. Now that's a public profession of faith! I know that impromptu baptism means that people may not get to tell their parents and invite their grandparents. But that's not really important. It may be important to the person, since I realize many want their family to share in the joy, but I don't see it as spiritually necessary. I believe it's a personal thing between the believer and his Lord. It's not some religious badge of achievement or acceptance that I need others to acknowledge —not even Mom. And sometimes, the desire to include and please family inappropriately supersedes or even replaces the desire to please Jesus. I've seen people postpone baptism for the sake of getting all the relatives to church on the same day, and end up waiting so long that they never get baptized at all.

Another time on a little family vacation at the beach, I decided to take a morning walk along the shore. As I walked, I noticed a man leaning on his car, apparently just waking up from an 'all nighter' in his car. I felt compassion for him, so I walked over and began to talk to him. He wanted to talk about cars and stereos and such, so I let him. But after about 15 minutes, I directed the conversation to his personal life and to Christ. I told him of the blessing of God and the power of salvation, and how God's will was good for him. He expressed how difficult things had been for him with family, work, and his alcohol problem. And after about an hour, I brought him around to the Door—Jesus. I asked if he was ready to open his heart to the Lord, and he got on his knees in the sand and prayed to be saved. He stood up happy and different, and immediately noticed something inside him—he said that he had no more desire to go to the store and buy more cigarettes and beer. Praise the Lord! He asked what he should do next. I looked over at the Gulf of Mexico and told him of water baptism. He readily agreed and we both entered the sea to dunk him in his only pair of clothes. I never saw him again after that, but I know that at least for a moment, he was on track with the Lord. Isn't that exciting?

What Words Do You Say?

Finally, what are you supposed to say as you baptize someone? It doesn't really matter. If the person being baptized understands that they are committing their life to Jesus Christ, then it counts. There are no formal statements that please God any more than others. Many have argued (and some denominations still do argue) that the right words must be said as the person goes under, or it doesn't count and they might need to get re-baptized. That is shallow and very spiritually childish to believe. If Jesus is the focus of the baptism, then you could just say, "Glory to God!" and dunk the person. Or you could just grunt and holler if you wanted to, and it would still count. Some have said that because Peter told some new converts to "be baptized in the name of the Lord Jesus Christ...", then we should say that. They go on to say that if you don't say that exact sentence, it didn't take. They also say that those who use the words that Jesus said, "baptizing them in the name of the Father, the Son, and the Holy Spirit..." are wrong for today. If you meet one of these people and they hear that you profess to be a Christian, the next statement out of their mouth will be "How did you get baptized? In the name of the Lord Jesus *only*?" And then they'll proceed to pour their pet doctrine on you (howbeit a false doctrine). Don't be moved.

When I baptize, I certainly like to say good words because words have power in them. I've chosen to say "In the name of the Lord Jesus Christ, I baptize you to the name of the Father, the Son, and the Holy Spirit..." I just put both scriptures in there so no one has to fight about it. I learned that from Kenneth Hagin, who made it through many hard decades of silly religious systems and doctrines, and who did it with great love and patience. I also like to pray for people's healing and deliverance at the same time if they have afflictions or pain. The water is a great point of contact that can help people open up their soul to receive a miracle from God.

Baptized in the Holy Spirit

After a person is born again, they also qualify to receive the baptism of the Holy Spirit and power. In Acts Chapter 8, after

Witness Principle 34

You Can Get Them Baptized in the Holy Spirit

Philip led many to receive Christ and be baptized in water, Peter and John joined him in Samaria and prayed for the new believers to receive the Spirit baptism. People will need to hear the truth about it before they have faith to receive this Spirit and power 'infilling' and their heavenly prayer language (tongues) that is evidence of it. So, if you feel they are open for more gospel truth and more of God, you can tell them some things. Instruct them that God wants the Holy Spirit, who has just entered them to abide forever, to come *upon* them with power. Explain to them that the only requirements are that they want Him to, and that they are ready to yield to the Spirit and allow Him to help them praise and speak in tongues. Why is this important? Because speaking and praying in tongues is the first supernatural moment where a Christian has yielded control to the Holy Spirit—control of his tongue.

The wonderful gifts of the Spirit are available to us, but the doorway is usually *tongues.* It seems that until we willingly yield to the Spirit in giving us utterance in tongues, we aren't really available for Him to use in other areas of power and manifestation (i.e. miracles, gifts of healings, words of knowledge, etc.). You don't have to give them a full Bible lesson on it. And if they seem hesitant, you can always just leave them with a seed of truth to be filled with the Spirit later.

But if they are open, just tell them to ask the Lord out loud to be filled with the Spirit and have their personal prayer language. Then touch their head or shoulder and ask the Lord to baptize them with the Holy Spirit and power. And then instruct them to "Think about God, and thank Him from your heart—but not with your own words—with *sounds* that He gives you, down in your spirit. Those sounds are the holy utterance (the language) the Spirit is giving, so let them float up. Let your tongue go a little, and give Him some voice until those sounds take over." Some people will instantly begin to speak in tongues, while others won't. If they do, explain that tongues is their new personal prayer language, and they can, and should, pray often in tongues. If they didn't, explain that there is more to learn, and that they should expect and desire the power of God to begin to work in their lives, and that He loves them greatly.

28
Know Your Word

Okay, now that you're all fired up and witnessing freely, I can go ahead and give you a theological challenge. It's time to know your Bible. It's time to be skillful with the Sword of the Spirit—the Word of God. Leading people to Jesus is fairly simple, as we've seen. But the Bible says to,

> **Study to show yourselves approved unto God, a workman that needeth not to be ashamed, rightly dividing the word of truth** (2 Timothy 2:15).
>
> **All Scripture is...profitable for doctrine...for reproof, for correction, for instruction...that the man of God may be complete, thoroughly equipped for every good work** (2 Timothy 3:16-17).

Basically, every believer ought to be able to answer basic questions on major Bible doctrines and explain things well enough to enlighten someone who doesn't know. True disciples will try and know most everything eventually, but here is a quick list to get you started. You'll need to study each one

> **Witness Principle 35**
>
> By Now, You Ought to Be Teachers

further, and you'll need to add other subject matter to your arsenal of understanding. Take notes in church, and spend some time at home arranging the truth inside your soul because you're going to encounter these spiritual questions soon.

1. *Why is Jesus the only way?* Jesus is the only way to God because sin disconnected us from God. Sin separated all humans from their Creator. Until sin is removed, God cannot come close to anyone. The only thing that removes sin from our account and from our heart is holy blood—a life for a life. Jesus died on the cross, shedding sinless blood, as payment for everyone's sin. Now, anyone who receives Him as their Savior and Sacrifice can be with God for eternity. No other religion has a proper "payment for sin" method. Asking for forgiveness, doing good to make up for bad, or doing religious activities is not enough.

2. *Can't I go to heaven just by being good? You know, I've never killed anyone, I haven't stolen much, and I don't cheat on my taxes.* That's not good enough. No one is good enough. There is only one way to be right with God, and it has nothing to do with an arbitrary measurement of how good people are. Jesus said that in order to enter to see God and enter His kingdom, "*ye must be born again*" (John Ch. 3). 'Born again' means that a person's spirit has come alive and is now connected to God. And it is the only way to be forgiven of sin.

3. *If God is good, why does He allow so many bad things to happen?* I've written the long answer in my book, *God, Why?* Really, the long answer is the only way to fill every crack of doubt that people have about God. And if people,

even believers, don't get their questions and doubts erased, their image of God will be cloudy and their faith will never get strong enough for the fight of faith. The short answer is that bad things happen for five categorical reasons: 1) Because this world has a glitch that weaved sin, affliction, and accidents into it. 2) Because people are destroyed for lack of knowledge. 3) Because of the devil. He is the killer, thief, and destroyer. 4) Because of the law of sin and death. Bad choices bring bad results. 5) Because people ignore the voice and leading of God. He may be speaking and directing us away from trouble, or to a solution, but we don't know how to hear His voice. The answer for why bad things happen is never "God had a reason." So, we must know how to bust the many spiritual myths about God such as: Myth #1—God is testing us. (No. He never tests anyone with evil or affliction.) Myth #2—God is in control of all things. (Nope. Only the good things.) Myth #3—The answer for every event is *God's will, God's will, God's will.* (Not true. For instance, God's will was for Adam and Eve to avoid the tree of knowledge and not ruin the world, but they did it anyway.) Myth #4—Everything happens for a divine reason. (Not really. Many things happen for a reason, but it's not always a divine reason.) Myth #5—God is punishing people and nations. (No, He's not. The wrath of God was satisfied at the cross until judgment day for the world, and now judgment has been given to Jesus for the Church.) All myths. All wrong. And all can be Biblically refuted.

4. *Water baptism and church attendance. Isn't being sprinkled as a baby and going to church a lot what gets me in?* Not at all. Water baptism was commanded by Jesus. He said, "*He who believes and is baptized shall be saved...*" That implies that a person must believe something first (believe the gospel) before being baptized. Baptism in water is only an outward display of an inward belief. It's the believing part that gets us in—not the baptism part. And babies haven't yet believed anything. Parents cannot make a salvation decision for their children. Parents can dedicate a baby to the Lord and promise to raise them in the church. But they cannot *choose* salvation for their baby. Everyone must choose Jesus Christ on their own, when they are old enough to understand. At what age do children understand? It's different for each. It's the day a child, not coerced but of their own volition, says to Dad, Mom, pastor or believer, something like, "I want Jesus in my heart." I say that as soon as a child wants to receive Christ, let them. Regardless of what's to happen in their future, help them awaken to God as early as possible so they can grow up with a conscience that is alive to God, and so their eternal destiny is secured.

   And going to church doesn't make someone a saved child of God either, no more than sitting in a garage makes someone a car. Church helps us learn and grow, but salvation comes only by a committed decision to receive Jesus Christ.

5. *What's the difference between all the Christian denominations?* The main difference is how closely their doctrine is guided by New Testament Scripture. First, to be considered a Chris-

tian denomination, salvation must be believed and preached as available to us through Jesus Christ alone. Only His blood sacrifice at the cross can restore us to God—no man made religious activities, no denominational stamp of approval, no shaking the preacher's hand, no water ritual, no circumcision, no 13 step obligation, no amount of praying or church attending, no confessions of sin, no singing of proper songs, no "this denomination is the only one that counts", and no praying for the dead can save a person.

This eliminates the Mormons and Jehovah Witnesses from the list, since they may acknowledge Jesus Christ in some manner, but they do not emphasize that He is the Way, the Truth, and the Life, that no man comes to the Father except through Him (John 14:6). But then again, this also eliminates even some denominations who don't preach it that way.

Other than salvation through Christ alone, the other big differences you will find have to do with the Holy Spirit, the power of God, and the authority of the believer. Many Christian denominations have made a decision to neglect the supernatural things of the New Testament, including laying hands on the sick, the baptism of the Holy Spirit and fire, speaking in tongues, and the faith and power of God for miracles. Why would they do that? Because spiritual, supernatural things challenge our natural minds. It's easier on the mind to believe that God does supernatural things all on His own without human involvement. But the Bible paints a different picture. All the miracles of God required a human element of faith and obedience. Even in Jesus' day, I'm sure people were very upset when Jesus spit on the blind man to heal him. Even though the man was healed, and even though good things happen today when people lay hands on the sick or speak in tongues, the unbelieving mind has a hard time with it.

I will not go into detail about all the different church beliefs. But I do acknowledge that when we are first saved, it is very natural to want to investigate and learn of them. As a matter of fact, the first book I searched for after my dedication to God was one on explaining all the differences of religions and denominations. What has happened with all these different church groups is no mystery. It happened in the early church as well. Paul addressed all the different factions and splits and called them all *babes in Christ*. But people are people. Man has this thing about wanting to create his own deal, devise his own pet doctrines, and raise his own, self-imposed flag of importance. And then, too, the devil helps deceive people into wrong theology. The only way to be safe and know exactly what God wants is to follow the New Testament and rightly divide the Word of Truth. There is a *right way* to understand the Bible, and it must be done with complete honesty and humbleness, majoring on the majors and minoring on the minors. And it must be done under the direction of the Spirit, *in* the Spirit, *with* the Spirit, and in the *spirit of the New Covenant*.

6. *The Bible was written by man and translated so many times, how can it be trusted?* The Bible was penned by man, but it was dictated by God, kind of like a boss saying to an assistant, "type

these words for me." The Bible says that all Scripture was given by inspiration of God, but that doesn't mean that God gave them "good feelings" and let them write what they wanted. The word 'inspire' means 'to breathe into'. God breathed the words into the prophets and apostles. So what we have is God's Word to the human race. I'm so glad—He wanted us to know Him, and He didn't leave us in the dark.

The Bible has been translated many times, but it is *not* a hand-me-down of translations where over time the meanings are lost and the last reads nothing like the original—not at all. Anyone who says that is *always and only* repeating something they heard someone else say because anyone who has ever read more than one Bible translation would admit that they all say basically the same thing, just with a few differences in word choice and phrase structure. The only reason for this popular rebuttal is that it gives sinners a hiding place from the truth. Maybe Mom or Dad used it. Or maybe they saw some nonsense on the History Channel. And it sounded like such an easy scapegoat to keep them out of religion that it was easy to adopt.

The Bible is *not* a hand-me-down of changes. Rather, each good translation of the Bible (some are definitely better than others) was accomplished by going back to the original Hebrew, Aramaic, and Greek words that were found hundreds of years ago on ancient scrolls and papers. The best Bibles are translations rather than interpretations. A translation is a word for word, language to language exchange, while an interpretation is when someone puts into their own words what they think is being said. For our reference Bibles and books, we can readily use interpretations and compare meanings. But for our main Bible, we all need a pure translation. I'll do my own word comparisons and meaning interpretations. But I want my text as close to the original as possible. And if need be, I can always go back to the Hebrew–Greek Interlinear, which contains the original wording, and do my own language study.

If you want my recommendations for Bible translations, they are these: the New King James and the New American Standard are my first choices, and they are somewhat similar. The Old King James was my favorite, and it's what I learned with. But the archaic Elizabethan language is difficult for many people, so for preaching, I reluctantly switched to the New King James, which is identical in most cases. Many people like the New International Version (NIV) because it is easy to read (it was written to be understood at the 7th grade level). However, the NIV is more an interpretation than a translation. And that makes it risky. It frequently loses the power and precision of key points and essential spiritual truths. So, in my opinion, it should not be used as anyone's primary Bible, nor should it be used as a study Bible. Only use it as a reference Bible or a Bible to leisurely read. I would even make a careful decision when giving it to children. Though they may like it because it's an easy read, remember that what children learn in their formative years will be what is stamped in their memory for decades to come. And we want that to be the more precise Bible scriptures rather than the 7th grade version. Granted, there are certain NIV scriptures that really interpret well and expand our understanding. But use it as just that—an interpretation and not a translation. Some scriptures in the NIV are incorrect, or even omitted. It is the same with the Living Translation and the New Living Translation. Use them as reference Bibles and not as your primary Bible. There are scores of other great Bible translations that help us clarify our understanding of certain scriptures, but I don't feel the need to mention them all.

29
Mistakes to Avoid

I want to share some error I've seen through the years concerning people's perceptions and motives in spreading the gospel.

To Those Going Through What I Went Through

One mistake I've noticed is to think that your main ministry and most effective witness will be to those just like you or to those who are going through what you went through. You know, the former alcoholic thinks he can best minister to alcoholics, or the former prisoner thinks he is automatically called back to the prison. It's not true. You may or may not be best at ministering to those following your path. Some of the greatest prison ministries are founded and led by preachers who never stepped a foot in prison until called to it. Think of Jesus. Jesus was never sick and afflicted, but he certainly ministered to those who were. Jesus was never crazy or possessed, but he easily set them all free. Paul the apostle was never married, but he still taught on marriage. It is wrong to teach that if someone needs help, they can only be helped by someone else who can relate to their exact situation. That's a natural, carnal belief, very deceptive, and can sometimes do more harm than good. The only thing that really solves problems is the power of God through the Word of God. And any Spirit-filled believer can give that. Sometimes, if the afflicted person knows you have been through the same thing they have, rather than strive to attain to the high mark of God's Word, they are relieved in their distress to know that you are like them. They begin comparing themselves to you or trying to mimic your walk and your points of success. And they miss God. Let's allow God's Spirit to be our guide for ministry, and let's not box Him into our preconceived, natural reasoning of *who is best for me to witness to.* If God speaks to you to go back to where you came from, then do it. But don't rationalize and force it just because you're more comfortable in "your home town" with your "homies."

I Must Be Called into Full-Time Ministry

Don't mistake your zeal for God and your holy fire for His kingdom (which *all* believers should have) for a call to formal full-time ministry. Being an effective soul-winner does not mean you're automatically an evangelist. You might be called into a certain five-fold office (Ephesians 4:11-12), but you might not. In order to stand in a leadership office of the Church, you're looking for the grace and gift of God, which is a decision made by the Lord. And you are waiting for the timing from Him. Many have thought they heard the voice of God on the matter, but they didn't test out the gift first and fell flat. If you are *not definitely* called into one of the five ministry offices of the Church, don't try to be. That's a road you don't want to go down. I've seen many well-meaning Christians fall in love with Jesus and with the gospel and wrongly assume that they must be called into a 'paid position' ministry. They feel the fire of God burning inside them, and they should. But that just means they're saved and full of the Spirit. We should all be *that*. We should all be totally sold out for the Lord and completely hungry and zealous all the days of our lives, but that doesn't determine our position in the Body, nor does it mean our livelihood must be from the gospel. Again, wrong motives and pursuits sometimes creep in on people who desire a better job, or who think that ministry work is easier or more fulfilling than secular work, or who desire more recognition or substantiation in life. Your vocation needs to be where God has assigned you, and nothing else.

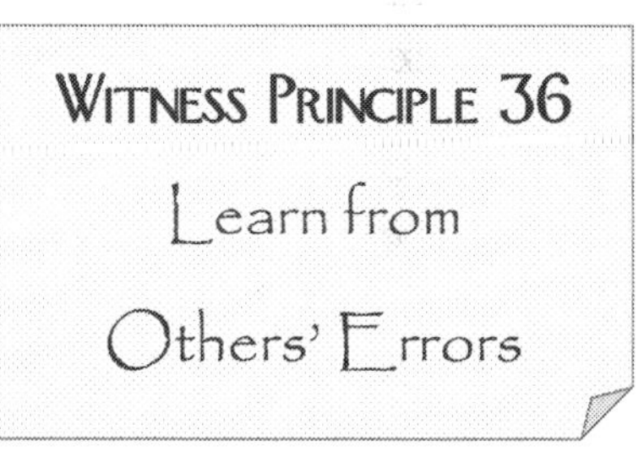

If you *are* called to one of the five preaching ministries, first, foremost, and forever, be faithful in your Christian call as a witness and servant, and God will open your additional calling door when it's time. (Yes, He will even inform your pastor if necessary. Your pastor is not your roadblock.) Never despise the value of a committed witness; remember, it is God whom we strive to please. And God doesn't view preachers as more special than believers. We are all equally "special" in Christ.

I Can Make More Money in the Gospel

No, you can't. If you're having trouble trusting God for finances *outside* the ministry, you'll have the same trouble (or more) *inside* the ministry. Don't look at ministry—soul-winning, preaching, or crusades—as a financial source. If you stay pure, and if you keep souls and ministry disconnected from your need for money, God will pay you. Those that preach the gospel can live of the gospel, but your heart must be right, or you'll mess it all up. Even if you're certainly called to a preaching office, you still need solid, relationship-based faith in God to care for you financially—not congregations, not offerings, not gospel products. Regardless of what business or ministry you are in, God must reside in your consciousness as the sole source for all blessing. Even a slightly wrong motive will ruin you.

The Cart Before the Horse

Don't put the cart before the horse. We who experience the power of God sometimes are so enamored with the greater works and the spectacular moments that we can forget the purpose—the same old, "un-spectacular" ministry of sharing our faith with a sinner and having someone repeat a prayer for salvation. We get excited about faith pioneers like Smith Wigglesworth, who raised the dead and cast demons and sicknesses out of people. But did you know that first, he was a soul-winner? We should all desire to walk in that same power. But did you know that the power he had was mixed in, as it should be, with the great commission? Here is what was said about Wigglesworth. If you want what *he* had, then want it *all*.

> **"Right through to old age, Wigglesworth sought the lost. There was a park near his home, and few people who frequented it were missed in his witnessing. He shared Christ with almost all he met, whether walking or riding."**

"Wigglesworth knew the excitement of great crusade meetings where he saw thousands come to the altar for salvation. But he never lost sight of the value of one soul. To the very last day of his life, he sought to win souls."

"His son-in-law wrote after his death, "He grew in grace and zeal for God, and his highest happiness was found in pointing others to the Lord Jesus. He tramped the country roads with that one purpose...To his dying day, he lived for this one thing, rarely coming home—morning, afternoon, or night—but what he had led someone to the Lord or ministered healing to a needy person"" (Wigglesworth, p. 88, 91, 93).

30

Why Would Anybody Reject Salvation?

Why would anyone reject this great salvation? People have given many excuses, but there's always something deeper—something they are hiding behind. Here are some real reasons for people rejecting our message of Jesus Christ.

1. The general reason is this: Satan has blinded them and they can't see the truth, no matter how loudly we preach it. "...if our gospel is veiled, it is veiled to those who are perishing, whose minds the god of this age has blinded, who do not believe, lest the light of the gospel of the glory of Christ, who is the image of God, should shine on them" (2 Corinthians 4:4). Every unsaved person is governed and clouded (sometimes more, sometimes less) by one of the "rulers of the darkness of this world" (Ephesians 6:12). Just in case you didn't know, Satan is the god of this world, not God. Jesus called the devil the "*ruler of the world*" or "*prince of this age*."

2. People who won't listen actually prefer to stay in the darkness. They are enjoying their Godless life. It is very similar to when a person is asleep in their home, and someone turns the light on in their bedroom. What is the startled person's reaction? "Turn off the lights!" You would think that anyone living a life in darkness would want to see where they were going. But they don't. They are comfortable in their darkness. They know the sinful layout of their life, and they are satisfied with it. "…the light has come into the world, and men loved darkness rather than light, because their deeds were evil. For everyone practicing evil hates the light and does not come to the light, lest his deeds should be exposed. But he who does the truth comes to the light, that his deeds may be clearly seen…" (John 3:19-21).

3. People prefer to be their own god rather than submit to a Higher One. When it comes down to it, the whole decision we all face is, *will I allow God to be Lord over me*? Or, am I determined to lord myself? From the Pharisees, who had prominence and power in religion, to the poorest, most feeble person, we detect a secret desire to be god. The saved one has decided to *lose his life* for Jesus, to bow in submission to his Creator. The unsaved, as well as the nominal Christian, thinks of *himself* as master. That's why the scriptures mention how hard it is for a rich man (who has money, power, and esteem) to humble himself and enter the kingdom. And how "…not many wise according to the flesh, not many mighty, not many noble, are called. But God has chosen the foolish things of the world to put to shame the wise" (1 Corinthians 1:26-27).

4. People are proud. They're proud of their family religious badge. They're proud of what their parents taught them. They're proud of their esteemed church name. Or they're proud of their self-absorbed opinion. And if what they are proud of is not the pure gospel, they are lost, and God won't draw them near.

5. People's hearts are not good ground. The parable of the sower in Mark Chapter 4 explains that when the Word is preached, you never know what type of heart it's falling on. Some Word falls on a careless heart, and Satan steals it. Some Word falls on stony ground, and though a person was glad to hear it at the time, they didn't move toward God, so it never took root. And some Word falls in the thorns, where the cares of this world, the deceitfulness of riches, and the desires for other things choke out the Word they heard. Finally, some hearts are good ground, and they become successful believers in Christ, some thirty-fold serious successful believers, some sixty-fold serious successful believers, and some one hundred-fold. So, three fourths of the hearts are not good ground. They are the ones who don't stick. They will acknowledge Jesus on a surface level, but they're not interested in Him. Don't be too surprised or disappointed in this. It's just the way it is. Prayer may sometimes help, but Jesus didn't really say that was the solution. He didn't give any solution. He just said that's how it is.

6. People have a wrong image of God. They still view Him as a cruel, unreasonable dictator, and they don't understand His good will for their lives. That keeps them bitter toward Him, and

that's why they need us. The devil hammers at them with *wrong* thinking. We deflect that hammer with *right* thinking.

31
How Do I Pray for the Lost?

Concerning prayer for the lost, let me first say that we need to develop a general concern for *all* lost people and keep a consistent prayer to God that His light will shine on their soul. This compassion keeps us in tune with the heart of God, opens the door for His anointing to be present in our lives, and allows us to be part of revival rather than just lethargic spectators. Picture what glory is experienced when a sinner turns to the Lord and begins to learn of God, and pray that everyone can experience that.

But next, because many Christians have long labored in prayer for their unsaved loved ones or friends, I want to improve our results with a couple of secrets on praying for *specific* people. Some have determined that *praying every day* for someone is the answer. So they do it. Some say that *deep intercession* is the only means of saving a lost loved one. So, they strive in tongues to get into a place of groaning and travail for their people. Some feel that all you have to do is *claim their salvation* and be done with it. And some feel that *if God wanted to save my people, He would do it without needing my prayer at all.*

But none of those are great answers. I will say that the best form of prayer for a lost person is the same as the best form of prayer in all situations—*faith-filled Holy Spirit-led prayer.* God knows the who, when, and how, better than we do. So allowing the Spirit to lead us and give us utterance in prayer is the key. If the Spirit were to have you pray for someone day after day, then I say do it. However, sometimes, those who are praying for family or close loved ones day after day, are doing it out of emotion, fear, and worry for the person. Or they are doing it out of obligation. That type of praying never works and only wastes time. If we are led by the Spirit, then God can impress upon us whom to pray for and when, and He will also let us know when we've prayed enough. If we're led by the Spirit, then God can even have us pray for someone besides our closest people. He may have us pray in tongues for someone we don't even know.

Sometimes, He leads us into a place of intercession, where we sense an intense tie to the soul of a person and a holy compassion of reconciling them to God. We stand as the link between them and Jesus, and we pray until it breaks, until we are at rest, until we know God has done something. But we can't force this type of praying. It is of the Spirit. We can't usually schedule an "intercessory prayer meeting" because we don't know exactly how the Spirit may lead in any particular prayer meeting. We can schedule a prayer meeting, and maybe we end up praying for the lost if that's how the Spirit leads. Or maybe we decide to have a meeting to pray for the lost, but it doesn't mean we will end up in deep intercession. Again, intercession is a spiritual working where the believer enters into the place of 'mediator' to bring people to Christ. And it is orchestrated by the Holy Spirit.

I've only had this happen to me a couple of times for people that I knew personally. One day, a friend of mine had come to my house to visit. As he was leaving, I watched his car drive off and around the corner. All of a sudden, I had this extreme burden of prayer come over me. I hit my knees on the driveway and began to weep for the man's soul with an extraordinary divine compassion. I felt myself both pleading with God for help and laying hold of salvation for my friend. This lasted for about two minutes, and then the burden lifted. I stopped crying, felt normal, and got off the ground. The peace of God came over me, and I began to laugh a little on the inside. I knew it was over. I knew that my friend would be opened to receive the Lord soon, and God would take hold of his life. Sure, I had prayed for all my friends, probably several times. And it is fine to pray for people as you wish. Praying for others keeps your heart in a right place and gives God a chance to do something. But on this occasion, I didn't force myself to get into a place of intercession. (When people force it, what they get is flesh and soul fervor, but no spirit power and no Holy Spirit operation.) This time of intercession was led by the Spirit, and it only took two minutes. Within three weeks, my friend was re-committed to the Lord. He was the one who came to me one freezing cold night to be baptized outside in the church water fountain.

Then it happened again—to another friend, the same way on the same driveway. Another one of my good friends came over. And as he was leaving, I watched his pickup truck drive off, and that same burden of prayer hit me. I prayed it through in about two minutes, and that same note of praise came over me. Sure enough, within one month, I had a chance to minister to him and help him rededicate to the Lord. Praise God. We need to be available for God to use in prayer. And sincere care for our fellow man is important.

But we must be careful not to get our emotions—our emotional, sensual, natural loving feelings—too involved, or it will mess up our praying and hinder more than help. Emotional "grip" can be the clear sign that we aren't really trusting God. The following is a story told by John G. Lake about a certain man with a wayward son. Though the man's decision sounds extreme, the spiritual catalyst is very important. Sometimes, a miraculous result requires an extreme decision in our own soul.

The Experience of Stephen Merritt

Stephen Merritt was a Godly old undertaker in the city of New York. His dear old wife and he had lived a Godly life. They had raised one son, and if there was ever a reprobate it was that son, Charley. Charley would get into some disreputable affair, and the police would come and say, "Charley has done so and so. It will take so much money to get him out of the difficulty." The next week another would come along with something else, and so it went on and on. And two old gray heads were praying and pouring out their tears for that boy's salvation.

One day as he sat in his office he was praying about his son, and the floor was wet with his tears, when he heard the voice of God saying, "How long have you been trying to save Charley?" So many of us are "trying to save Charley," and we have gotten in the way of the Lord. He replied: "Lord, a long time." The Lord said, "Now if you are through, I will undertake." The old man considered, and it worked out in his soul this way.

The police came and said, "Charley did so and so."

He asked, "Who is Charley?"

"Why he is your son."

"No, I have no son Charley." That day as he knelt there he said, "Lord, he is not my son anymore. I give him over to you until he is saved." So he told police, "No, I have no son." They looked at him and shook their heads. Then they sent another officer. But it was no use to go to him anymore. It looked as if the old man had gone crazy.

About nine months passed, and one day an officer came and said: "Charley has jumped off the Brooklyn Bridge and finished." He wanted the old man to have the river dragged to obtain the body. But said, "Oh, no, I have no son, Charley. Drag the river if you want to." So they dragged the river, but the body they found was not Charley's. Three months more passed, and one day a clerk said, "There is one of your friends in the office." And when he came in it was Charley. He was beautifully dressed, clean faced, everything indicating the light of God, and when the old father came in, the son fell at his feet, kissed them, and asked his forgiveness. He said in explanation, "Three months ago I was saved in a mission, but I did not want to come and see you until I came as a man."

The Human Clutch

Not only is it so in your prayers for others, but in your prayers for yourself, some of you are holding to your sickness, or difficulty, with such a clutch, and are so everlastingly conscious of it, that God cannot get it out of your hands. You are in the very place spiritually where old Stephen Merritt was. He was so determined to save his boy that he was just doing it himself, and God was not getting a chance.

Open your hands, let go of the old difficulty. I was praying for a woman who had appendicitis, and as I prayed I saw she was holding on to it mentally so hard I had to do something. So I told one of the craziest stories I ever told, and finally she burst out laughing in spite of the pain, and when she got through the pain was gone. She just opened her clutch (Lake, p. 335-337).

Notice what the Lord said to Stephen, "…now if you are through, I will undertake." God just wanted him to let go of the care. Jesus said that "whatsoever you bind on earth is bound in heaven; whatsoever you loose on earth is loosed in heaven" (Matthew 18:18). Some people have so bound themselves to the worry of a loved one, that heaven is bound in helping. Stephen Merritt loosed himself from his emotional clutch on his son and let God take over. That's the point.

My wife, Joni, gives an example of this in her praying for her nephew. He had gone through some tough times of affliction and distance from God, and Joni had poured her heart out to God for him in prayer many times. At first, her praying was in the Spirit, and it was effective. But then it turned emotional. One day in prayer, the Spirit of the Lord fell on her for a brief moment and she interceded for her nephew. But after it lifted, she admits that she kept on praying for about 15 minutes, all in the flesh, very emotionally in her soul. Then the Lord spoke to her and said, "I can't use you to pray about this anymore. You're too emotional." And that was it. That ended her praying for him for about two years. She had no grace, no power, and no leading to pray for him—for a two year "suspension." After the two years, her soul was disconnected enough, and she was able to address her nephew again in prayer. About the same time, her father, who was "keeping it before the Lord" (that's the lingo we use when we're really just still quite anxious), also found the secret of casting the care to the Lord and disconnecting from the emotional strain of it. And shortly thereafter, the blessing came—her nephew was saved, delivered, and on a better road. By following God's leading in prayer of who, when and how, and by cutting off from the emotional distress of it, we can avoid many unfruitful hours, months, and years of praying. And we can get better results.

Right Praying Avails Much

1. Talk to God. Verbalize your desire for people.
2. Don't forget to pray for the lost, in general, rather than only your closest family.
3. When you pray, don't ask God to save them. (He has already done all He's going to do to save people. He provided salvation for all.) Rather, ask Him to open their soul to believe.
4. Believe that God is hearing, that He wants them saved, too, and that He will begin working on them now.
5. Be led by the Spirit of whom, when, and how to pray.
6. Maybe you get into a place of intercession, but maybe you don't. Just pray with the Spirit.
7. You can address the devil and command the darkness to flee a person's mind (this works if you are in a place of authority in that person's life).
8. You can pray the written Spirit-led prayers in the Bible for people (Ephesians 1:15-19, 3:14-20, Colossians 1:9-12).
9. At some point, you must release your clutch on a person. Cast the burden off your soul and let God take over.
10. Ask God to send other effective laborers into their path.
11. Finally, we cannot simply "claim salvation" for someone.

32
THE MAIN THING

Certainly, the love commands are the main thing. And certainly, living by faith and understanding this new covenant with God is the main thing. But our work at hand is also the main thing. The great commission is really the *only* commission, and it is the main thing. If we catch the spirit of the New Testament and the pure, high calling of God, we'll be safe and successful. However, if we're distracted with winds of doctrine or deceived into "heaping teachers to ourselves", we will effectively cover up and overshadow our assignment.

> **WITNESS PRINCIPLE 37**
>
> The Main Thing Is to Keep the Main Thing the Main Thing

And the holy power we received to be witnesses will leak out.

Jesus pointed a finger at the early Church at Ephesus and rebuked them. He said,

> **I have this against you, that you have left your first love. Remember therefore from where you have fallen; repent and do the first works, or else I will come to you quickly**

and remove your lampstand from its place unless you repent (Revelation 2:4-5).

People have long guessed at what this first love and first works were. But I believe I found it. Acts Chapter 19 is the first mention of this Ephesus assembly, where Paul journeys for the first time and found some disciples who didn't know anything about Jesus or the Holy Spirit. He preached and prayed, they were saved and filled with the Spirit, and then he "...withdrew the disciples, reasoning daily in the school of Tyrannus. And this continued for two years, so that *all who dwelt in Asia heard the word* of the Lord Jesus, both Jews and Greeks" (Acts 19:9,10). Did you catch it? What evidence do we have of the Ephesus church's first love and first works? The whole country of Asia heard the Word during this two year period, so the Ephesus church must have been *spreading the Word.* Whether they invited people to the school or told them of Jesus personally, the Word of God made it to every single citizen. I believe Jesus was commanding them to get back to that original love for God (first love) and zeal for telling others (first works).

Terry Mize consistently reminds the Church that we've got a missionary call from *heaven*—Jesus commanded us. We've got a missionary call from *hell*—the burning rich man wanted someone to go warn his family. And we've got a missionary call from *earth*—the man from Macedonia. Everyone needs the gospel. And everyone's calling us. We can go overseas. And, I say we can also go into our backyard and preach over the fence to our neighbor.

One time I was a guest at a certain church. Before service, I was sitting in the pastor's office, waiting for him, when through the door, I heard a conversation in the office lobby. Two visiting teenagers had accidentally walked in the wrong church door and found themselves in the office area. At the same time, one of the church elders happened to walk into the office area, and saw the teenagers. He pounced, but not in the right way. He sharply rebuked them for being in the office, and wasn't very accepting as they tried to apologize. He sent them out to go around to the correct door, and so he and they left. I knew something was wrong, though, from the exchange I had heard. I jumped up and ran out of the pastor's office and outside, only to see the two boys walking off, going home to their apartments around the corner. I yelled over to them to greet them and wave them back. When I did, they turned and began arguing to one another. One of the boys wanted to come back, but the other didn't because he didn't feel welcome. They talked a few seconds, and split from each other. The one came back, telling his friend to go on home if he wanted. David came to church by himself for the first time in his life and gave his life to Jesus that night. From that day, he began attending the church regularly—by himself—no parents, no friend. He was soon filled with the Spirit and began living his life for God. Praise the Lord. What happened here? We got one of the boys, but we might have lost one because the church elder had forgotten to keep the main thing the main thing.

It's time to repent and do the first works. We have allowed the education of the Christian to be his only goal. But education for education's sake is never complete. We have implied that the only requirement from sheep is to come to church, open their mouths to be fed the Word, and give tithes and offerings. I agree that sheep must first get hungry and stay hungry for the Word of God. And they certainly should be giving their supply of money for the work. But, really, we should soon teach them how to also *feed themselves* and then to work off the "calories" out in the hurting world. You've heard the analogy—that a sheep that gets fat and has too much wool will tip over and can't get up without the shepherd's help. We shepherds in the Church can easily spend all our time helping fallen sheep if we don't emphasize what they are to work toward.

The Church can't allow itself to remain a perfectly restored classic car that is never driven, but only waxed, oiled, gassed, shined, revved up in the garage for all our friends, and then repeated every week. Let's hit the road, Jack! The Body of Christ must not be an army that trains and trains and trains but never goes to war. We are not only an infirmary where the hurting can be repaired, but instead, where the repaired are trained for battle and directed to the field. The pastor cannot be a shepherd who puts a sign on the gate of the pasture with a bowl of food trying to lure sheep in. But, instead, his role is to prepare the sheep to begat their own sheep. And since you are a sheep, it's time to "begat."

Church-wide event evangelism has a certain place. It is good to work together on large scale projects to bring sinners into meetings. But let's not imply that the grand events are, in any way, a substitute for personal evangelism. In our world, it takes something more than gospel musicals and stage performances to *consistently* impact sinners. I encourage every believer, every month, every week, every day, to let the Holy Spirit use you in the real, old fashioned gospel way of *you shall receive power...and you shall be witnesses.*

God gave Jesus to the world. Jesus gave the gospel to His disciples. They gave the gospel to others. Those others gave the gospel to someone else. And eventually, someone gave the gospel to you. Out of the thousands of people you will influence in this life, who will you give it to?

Bibliography

Norvel Hayes, *The Ministry for Everyone*, 1983, Norvel Hayes, p. 9

John G. Lake, *His Life, His Sermons, His Boldness of Faith*, 1994, Kenneth Copeland Publications, p. 529

Dr. Bob Moorehead, *The Fellowship of the Unashamed*, 2012, http://www.godswork.org/inspiration6.htm

Inspiring Quotes to Live By, 2012, http://www.soulwinning.info/gs/quotes.htm

Smith Wigglesworth, *Ever Increasing Faith*, 1971, Gospel Publishing House, p. 99

Bob Laurent, *Watchman Nee*, 1998, Barbour Publishing, p.100-103

Charles Finney, *Revivals of Religion*, 1978, CBN University Press

George Stormont, *Wigglesworth*, 1989, Harrison House, p. 88, 91, 93

Michael Shank, The Atheist and His Conscience, http://ezinearticles.com/?The-Atheist-and-His-Conscience&id=2725604

About the Author

Rev. Chas Stevenson is a stimulating Bible teacher and author of the life-changing book, *God, Why?* He and his wife, Joni are founders of *Stevenson Ministries*, and founders and pastors of *Houston Faith Church*, an exciting and growing church in Houston, Texas. Chas' ministry to the Church at large is marked with a refreshing demonstration of God's Word and power that quiets the emotions, stirs the spirit, and brings people back to their high calling of God in Christ. With New Testament, scriptural logic that feels like bowling balls crashing through glass pins, Chas is a foundation builder of God's Word in people, holding nothing back in igniting people's faith toward God while keeping false doctrine and common Christian distractions exposed by the Word of God.

After leaving his business systems consulting career in 1997, Chas began serving the Lord with a powerful and refreshing evangelistic and healing gift, igniting churches and training believers to win souls and heal the sick. For several years, he worked with Angelo Mitropoulos in R.W. Schambach's tent meetings in the inner cities of America, coordinating street ministry and seeing multitudes saved, healed, and delivered from demons. Since then, he has successfully imparted into church members an attitude of personal soulwinning and world evangelism that keeps believers glued to the primary call of the Christian and will ultimately help them earn a "well done, thou good and faithful servant..." from the Lord.

Made in the USA
Columbia, SC
30 June 2025

59974426R00133